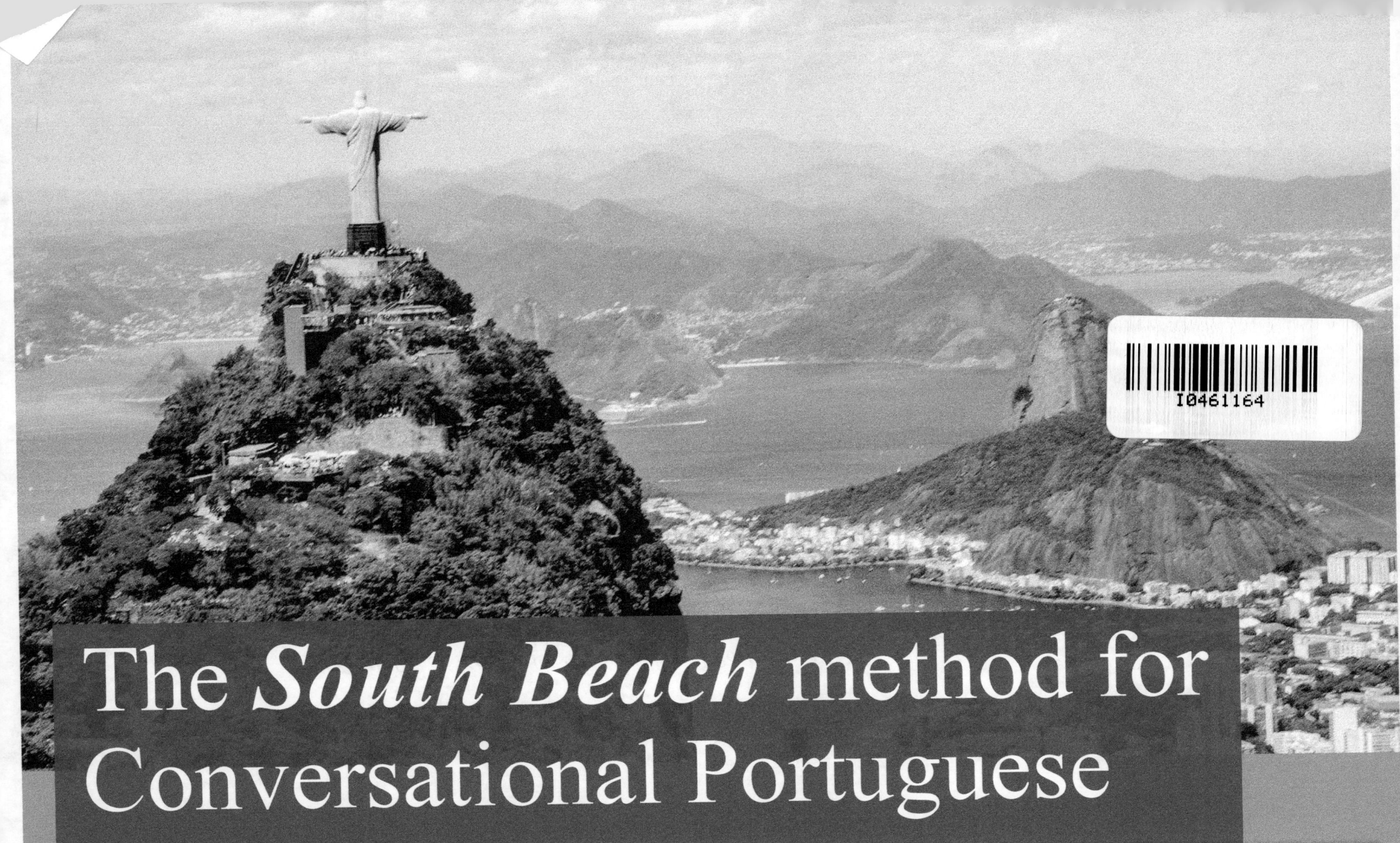

The *South Beach* method for Conversational Portuguese

By: Erasmus-Cromwell Smith

ISBN: 979-8-9866136-3-5

Publisher: Erasmus Press
Editor and Proofreading: Elisa Arraiz Lucca
Cover Design and Interior Design: Abjini Shamanik
www.erasmuscromwellsmith.com

This course is radically different from any others as you will be taking steps backwards to revisit a bit of English Grammar in order to refresh certain rules and practices of our language.

As you will see, there are plenty of things we say simply because we are used to but on many of them, we don't know whether they are right or even why we speak that way.

The premise is simple, we go back and revisit our language to refresh or learn certain concepts to translate English properly into Portuguese. Our own language construction has to be grammatically right (properly built), otherwise what will come out in Portuguese will be equally wrong!

Conversational Portuguese

➤ This course will enable you to speak Portuguese within hours.

➤ This course debunks the idea that Portuguese is a very hard language to learn.

➤ Actually, in most cases, both languages are spoken in the same way (literally like a mirror image).

➤ The Foundation of this method is the Infinitive Verbs.

➤ You will learn to speak through 4 templates (all of them using Infinitive Verbs).

➤ The method also teaches you how to pronounce/spell properly in Portuguese.

➤ It also allows/ enables you to study/learn most Portuguese Verbs only in Infinitive Form (almost without conjugations) effectively cutting thousands of hours and thousands of verb conjugations from the learning process.

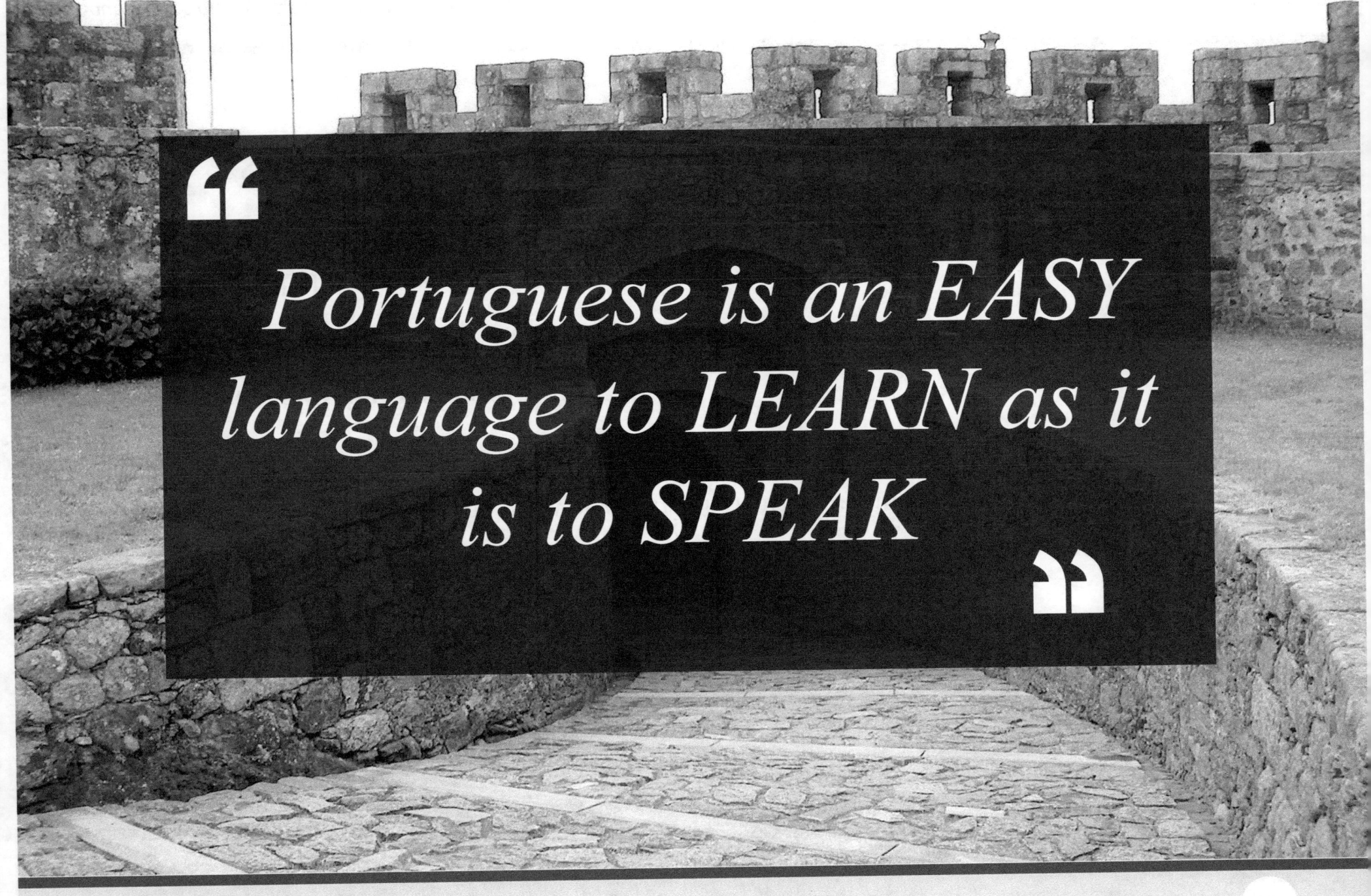

> **Portuguese is an EASY language to LEARN as it is to SPEAK**

Let Us Begin

For the most part :

➢ Portuguese is spoken the same way English is!

➢ Most of the grammar rules (even their names) are the same.

➢ Phrases are structured the same way.

➢ Many, many words are very similar if not the same.

Portuguese **difficulty debunked:**

➢ Portuguese vowels have only one sound:

➢ English has two or more sounds per vowel!

So, let's debunk the idea that Portuguese is so difficult!

Learning Step 1

Everything Begins With

The 5 Vowels

Next you will learn how to pronounce them easily!

Lesson 1: Part 1

The Basics First "The Vowels"

Portuguese Vowel	Portuguese Pronunciation Easy: Pronunciation is in parenthesis ( )					
	Repeat	Again	Again	Again	Again	Again
A (Ah)	(Ah)	(Ah)	(Ah)	(Ah)	(Ah)	(Ah)
E (Eh)	(Eh)	(Eh)	(Eh)	(Eh)	(Eh)	(Eh)
I (Ee)	(Ee)	(Ee)	(Ee)	(Ee)	(Ee)	(Ee)
O (Oh)	(Oh)	(Oh)	(Oh)	(Oh)	(Oh)	(Oh)
U (Oo)	(Oo)	(Oo)	(Oo)	(Oo)	(Oo)	(Oo)

Now let's practice them one after the other:

Now do it faster: **Ah-Eh-Ee-Oh-Oo**   now even faster: **Ah-Eh-Ee-Oh-Oo**

Keep on practicing : **Ah-Eh-Ee-Oh-Oo** until you memorize it

Repeat and memorize the sound.
Try to do it faster & faster.

Learning Step 2

Next is to learn

The Alphabets

Pronunciation in Portuguese is in (parenthesis)!

Lesson 1: Part 2

Pronunciation and phonetics of the Portuguese Alphabet

A (Ah)	B (bh)	C (zeh)	D (deh)	E (eh)	F (ef)
G (jeh)	H (*silent*)	I (ee)	J (jeh)	K (kahh)	L (ehl)
M (em)	N (en)	O (oh)	P (peh)	Q (koo)	R (ehrreh)
S (es)	T (teh)	U (oox)	V (veh)	W (duplo v)	X (zeh/sh/ehs)
Y (ee grega)		Z (zehtah)			

Learning Step 2

It is also very useful to learn

The Numbers

Lesson 1: Part 3

Um	Dois	Três	Quatro	Cinco	Seis	Sete	Oito	Nove
One	Two	Three	Four	Five	Six	Seven	Eight	Nine
Dez	Vinte	Trinta	Quarenta	Cinquenta	Sessenta	Setenta	Oitenta	Noventa
Ten	Twenty	Thirty	Forty	Fifty	Sixty	Seventy	Eighty	Ninety

Cem One hundred	**Duzentos** Two hundred	**Trezentos** Three hundred	**Quatrocentos** Four hundred
Quinhentos Five hundred	**Seiscentos** Six hundred	**Setecentos** Seven hundred	**Oitocentos** Eight hundred
Novecentos Nine hundred	**Mil** One thousand	**Dez mil** Ten thousand	**Cem Mil** One hundred thousand
Um milhão One million	**Cem mil milhões** One hundred million	**Um bilhão** One billion	**Um trilhão** One trillion

Learning Step 3

Having learned the alphabet and the vowels, the next step is to learn:

The Nouns

Lesson 2: Part 1

I – You	
	Easy , just read it !
Read it aloud I – **Eh-oo**	Read it aloud You – **Vohceh/Too**
Read it aloud I – **Eh-oo**	Read it aloud You – **Vohceh/Too**
Read it aloud I – **Eh-oo**	Read it aloud You – **Vohceh/Too**
Read it aloud I – **Eh-oo**	Read it aloud You – **Vohceh/Too**
Read it aloud I – **Eh-oo**	Read it aloud You – **Vohceh/Too**
Read it aloud I – **Eh-oo**	Read it aloud You – **Vohceh/Too**
Read it aloud I – **Eh-oo**	Read it aloud You – **Vohceh/Too**
Read it aloud I – **Eh-oo**	Read it aloud You – **Vohceh/Too**

*Remember in Portuguese <u>I</u> is **Eh-oo**, <u>You</u> is **Voceh**.*

He – She

Easy , just read it !

Read it aloud He – **Ehleh**	Read it aloud She – **Ehlah**
Read it aloud He – **Ehleh**	Read it aloud She – **Ehlah**
Read it aloud He – **Ehleh**	Read it aloud She – **Ehlah**
Read it aloud He – **Ehleh**	Read it aloud She – **Ehlah**
Read it aloud He – **Ehleh**	Read it aloud She – **Ehlah**
Read it aloud He – **Ehleh**	Read it aloud She – **Ehlah**
Read it aloud He – **Ehleh**	Read it aloud She – **Ehlah**
Read it aloud He – **Ehleh**	Read it aloud She – **Ehlah**

*Remember in Portuguese <u>He</u> is **Ehleh**, <u>She</u> is **Ehlah***

Lesson 2: Part 2

We – You	Easy , just read it !
Read it aloud We – **Nohs**	Read it aloud You – **Vohs**
Read it aloud We – **Nohs**	Read it aloud You – **Vohs**
Read it aloud We – **Nohs**	Read it aloud You – **Vohs**
Read it aloud We – **Nohs**	Read it aloud You – **Vohs**
Read it aloud We – **Nohs**	Read it aloud You – **Vohs**
Read it aloud We – **Nohs**	Read it aloud You – **Vohs**
Read it aloud We – **Nohs**	Read it aloud You – **Vohs**
Read it aloud We – **Nohs**	Read it aloud You – **Vohs**

*Remember in Portuguese <u>We</u> is Nohs, <u>You</u> is **Vohs***

They – It		Easy , just read it !
Read it aloud They – **Ehlehs, ehlahs**	Read it aloud It – **Eessoh**	
Read it aloud They – **Ehlehs, ehlahs**	Read it aloud It – **Eessoh**	
Read it aloud They – **Ehlehs, ehlahs**	Read it aloud It – **Eessoh**	
Read it aloud They – **Ehlehs, ehlahs**	Read it aloud It – **Eessoh**	
Read it aloud They – **Ehlehs, ehlahs**	Read it aloud It – **Eessoh**	
Read it aloud They – **Ehlehs, ehlahs**	Read it aloud It – **Eessoh**	
Read it aloud They – **Ehlehs, ehlahs**	Read it aloud It – **Eessoh**	
Read it aloud They – **Ehlehs, ehlahs**	Read it aloud It – **Eessoh**	

*Remember in Portuguese <u>They</u> is **Ehlehs, ehlahs**, <u>It</u> is **Isso***

Lesson 2: Part 2

Summary	The Nouns	Easy, just read it! ()
Let's continue to practice!	I – **Eh-oo**	Repeat it 5 times!
	You – **Vohceh/Too**	Repeat it 5 times!
	He – **Ehleh**	Repeat 5 more times
	She – **Ehlah**	This one 5 times as well
	We – **Nohs**	Pronounce this one 5 times
	You – **Vohs**	This one 5 times as well
	They – **Ehlehs, ehlahs**	5 times with this as well
	It – **Eessoh**	This one 5 times as well

Learning Step 4

The following are essential to any conversation:

Magic Words

Practice them!

Lesson 3: Part 1

Let us introduce a few words that are essential in any conversation.

An/A = **um (oom)**	Yes = **sim (seem)** No = **não (nahoh)**
The = **o (oh)**	At = **em (ehm)**
And = **e (eh)**	To = **para (pahrah)**
With = **com (kom)**	That = **que (keh),** **este (ehsteh),** **aquele (ah-kooehleh)**
Or = **ou (oo)**	This = **isto (Eestoh)**

Lesson 3: Part 1

What = **o que, o quê**	But = **mas**
When = **quando**	Whose = **de quem**
Where = **onde**	Who = **quem**
Why/ Because = **porque, porquê**	Which = **qual**
Whether = **se**	How = **como**
To = **para**	For = **por, para**
From = **de, do, a partir de**	While = **enquanto, durante**
How many = **quantos**	Whom = **quem**
For = **por, para**	As = **como**
More than = **mais do que**	How Much = **quanto**

Lesson 3: Part 2

A

A: um
About To: prestes a
Against: contra
Although: apesar de, embora
And: e
As...As: Tão ...como
At (place): em
At What Time: a que horas
A Little: um pouco
Above: acima
Ago: atrás, anteriormente
Already: já
And Now, What: e agora
As Long As: enquanto
At (hour): em, no
Awful: horrível, terrível, horroroso
A Little Bit: um pouco
After: depois
All: tudo
Also: também
Another: outro, outra

As Soon As: assim que
At this Moment: neste momento
A Lot: muito
Afterwards: mais tarde
All Day: todo o día
Always: sempre
Anybody: qualquer um
About: sobre
Again: outra vez, de novo
Almost: quase
Amusing: divertido
As: como
Appointed: nomeado
At This Time: a esta hora

B

Barely: Por pouco
Between: entre
Butter: manteiga
Because: porque
Bit: bocado
By: por

Before: antes
Both: ambos
By The Way: a propósito
Behind: atrás de
Breakdown: antes
Below: embaixo de
But: mas

C

Careful: Ter cuidado
Caution: cautela
Certain: certo
Careful: cuidado
Caution: cautela
Certain: certo

D

Dear: querido(a)
Difficult: difícil
Departure: partida
Despite: embora

Lesson 3: Part 2

Detour: desvio
Divided By: dividido por

F

Fair: justo
Fine: bom
Further: além disso
Far: longe
For: para
Fault: culpa
For The Reason: pela razão
Feasible: viável
Few: poucos
From: de

G

Generally: geralmente
Good: bom

H

Half: metade, meio

How Long: por quanto tempo
Heavy: pesado
How Much: quanto
How: como
Hot: quente

I

If: se
Impossible: impossível
In front of: diante de
In good health: em boa saúde
Inside: dentro
It is necessary: é preciso
Immediately: imediatamente
Improbable: improvável
In case of: em caso que
In order that: para que
Instead of: em vez de
It could be: poderia ser
In: em

In case that: em caso que
In order to: para
In spite of: a pesar de
It maybe: pode ser
Important: importante
In a hurry: com pressa
Included: incluído
In the habit of: no hábito de
Interesting: interessante

J

Just: somente

K

Keep: guardar
Kind: gentil

L

Lacking: faltando
Latest: ultimo
Least: menos

Lesson 3: Part 2

Likely: provável
List: lista
Low: baixo
Large: grande
Left: deixar
Little: pequeno
Last: ultimo
Leftover: sobra
Long: longo
Late: tarde
Looks Like: parece
Later: mais tarde
Less: menos
Late: tarde
Looks Like: parece
Later: mais tarde
Less: menos

M

Made In: fabricado em
Mrs.: Sra.

Many: muitos
Much: muito
Maybe: pode ser, talvez
Merely: apenas
Miss.: senhorita
More: mais

N

Named (to be): nomeado (a ser)
Neither: nenhum
Nothing: nada
Narrow: estreito
Never: nunca
Now: agora
Near: aproximar
New: novo
Nearby: perto
Next: próximo
Necessary: necessário
Next to: ao lado de, perto de
Not: não

O

Obvious: obvio
On: sobre
Open: aberto, abrir
Outside: fora
Odd: ímpar
On Call: em chamada
Or: ou
Over: sobre
Of: do
Once: uma vez
Other: outro
Overcome: superar
Of course: é claro
Ongoing: em andamento
Otherwise: caso contrario
Overlook: omitir, deixar passar
Often: muitas vezes, freqüentemente

Lesson 3: Part 2

Only: apenas
Out: fora

P

Percent: por cento
Point: ponto
Push: empurre
Perhaps: talvez
Probable: provável
Pleasant: agradável
Problem: problema
Perfectly: perfeitamente
Program: program
Please: por favor
Pull: puxar

Q

Question: pergunta
Quite Enough: bastante

R

Ready: preparado

Repeat: repetir
Routine: rotina
Regularly: regularmente
Right Away: agora mesmo
Responsible: responsável
Right Now: agora mesmo
Ridiculous: ridículo
Relative: relativo

S

See you Later: até logo
Sir: senhor
Something: algo
Still: ainda
Several: diversos
So: então
Somewhat: um pouco
Stop: para, pare
Show Me: mostra-me
Some: algum
So Much: tanto
Subject: sujeito

Side: lado
Somebody: alguém
Soon: em breve
Sure: claro
Similar: semelhante
Someone: alguém
Specific: específico
Somewhere: em algum lugar

T

Task: tarefa
The: o
Together: juntos
Too (also): também
There Will Be: haverá
That: este
There: lá
Through: pela
Those: aqueles
Therefore: portanto

Lesson 3: Part 2

There: lá
These: esses
To: para
Too Much: muito
There is/are: existe/são
Thick: grosso, espesso
Tomorrow: amanhã
This Evening: esta noite
There Have Been: houve
This: isto, este
Thing: coisa
Tonight: esta noite
There was/were: houve/foram
There Would Be: haveria

U

Underneath: por baixo
Unlikely: acima
Unwilling: relutante
Under: debaixo
Up: acima
Until: até
Useful: util

Understood: entendido
Unless: a não ser que
Unfortunately: infelizmente
Unpleasant: desagradável

V

Very: muito

W

Warm: caloroso
Why: por que
Where To: para onde
Without: sem
With: com
Whatever: qualquer que seja
Whereby: pelo que, por meio de
Whoever: quem
Watch Out: preste atenção
Wide: largo
Who: quem
With Me: comigo
Whether: se

Well: bem
Which: que, qual
With you: contigo
Whole: todo
Whereabouts: paradeiro
Wet Paint: tinta fresca
What: o que
When: quando
Where: onde
Whenever: em qualquer momento
Which: que
With you: contigo
Within: dentro de
While: enquanto
Who: quem
Whole: todo
Without: sem
Whose: de quem

Y

Yet: ainda
Yield: colheita

Learning Step 5

Reflexes and Possessives

are essential to complete a sentence

Practice them, emphasize the pronunciation

Lesson 3: Part 3

Reflexive

Me – **Me**	Call me	**chama-me**
You – **Te**	Bring you	**trazer-te**
Him – **Le**	Take him	**leva-o**
Her – **La**	Invite her	**convidá-la**
Us – **Nos**	Get us	**pegue-nos**
You – **Les**	Buy for you	**comprar-te**
Them – **Les**	Write them	**escreve-os**
It – **Lo**	Sell it	**vendé-lo**

Examples:

You	have	to go	to take him	home
Tens	**de**	**ir**	**levá-lo à casa**	
He	can	come	to see me later	
Ele	**pode**	**vir**	**ver-me mais tarde**	
They	want	to bring	her to see you	
Ele	**quer**	**trazê-la**	**para te ver**	
They	are	trying	to call today	
Eles	**estão**	**tentando**	**chamar hoje**	

Possessive

My – **Meu/minha**	My home	**Minha casa**
Your – **Teu/tua**	Your car	**Teu carro**
His – **Seu**	His son	**Teu filho/ tua filha**
Her – **Sua**	Her pet	**Sua mascot**
Our – **Nosso/a**	Our boat	**Nosso barco**
Your – **Vosso/a/s**	Your dad	**Teu pai**
Their – **Deled/delas**	Their idea	**Sua ideia**
Its – **Sua**	Its tail	**Sua cauda**

Examples:

You	are	welcome to	our	house
	Es	**bem-vindo à**	**nossa**	**casa**
She	is	driving	my	car
Ela	**está**	**conduzindo**	**meu**	**carro**
They	want	to take	my	wife
Eles	**querem**	**levar a**	**minha**	**esposa**
Today	I want	to go	to my	studio
Hoje	**eu quero**	**ir ao**	**meu**	**estúdio**

Lesson 3: Part 3

Notes on Reflexives : In Portuguese a reflexive can also be placed right after the noun (at the very beginning of the phrase), it is preferable this way.

Examples :

I will bring them home
Eu vou trazê-los para casa

I want to take him to the airport
Eu quero levá-lo para o Aeroporto

I have to go to purchase the medicines for him
Eu tenho de ir comprar os medicamentos para ele.

I can prepare de food for you at twelve
Eu posso preparar a comida para ti às doze.

Learning Step 6

The Infinitive Verbs

Are the foundation of this course they are used almost identically both in English and Portuguese

Practice them!

Lesson 4: Part 1

What is an Infinitive Verb?

1) Well, it starts with a "To" in English and ends with a "**r**" in Portuguese

   Example: to call to come to go to eat

   chamar **vir** **ir** **comer**

2) It's never the 1st. verb (as it can't be conjugated)

   You can't say in English ~~I to call~~ ~~I to come~~ ~~I to go~~ ~~I to eat~~

   You can't say in Portuguese ~~Eu chamar~~ ~~Eu vir~~ ~~Eu ir~~ ~~Eu comer~~

3) But it's always used after the 2nd. Infinitive Verb.

   Example:

   I want to go to eat.

   Eu **quero** **ir** **comer.**

   She wants to come to visit.

   Ela quer **vir** **visitar.**

Lesson 4: Part 2

This course is built around the Infinitive Verbs

In English, infinitive verbs are used all the time:

I want to go to eat now.

He wants to come to visit you.

In Portuguese Infinitive Verbs are used the the same way

All the time and in the same way we do !

I	want	to go	eat	now.
Eu	**quero**	**ir**	**comer**	**agora.**

He	wants	to come	visit you.
Ele	**quer**	**vir**	**te visitar.**

SMILE ☺ *Both sentences mirror each other.*

Lesson 4: Part 3

This course is built around **the Infinitive Verbs**

Here are more examples!

I **Eu**	have **tenho**	to take you **de levar-te**	She **Ela**	wants **quer**	to watch TV **assistir TV**	till midnight **até a meia noite**
You **Tú**	have **tens**	to bring him **que trazê-lo**	We **Nós**	want **queremos**	to go to shop **ir à loja**	at noon **ao meio dia**
He **Ele**	has **tem**	to go to see you **que ir ver-te**	They **Eles**	want **querem**	to give you **dar-te uma**	a surprise **surpresa**
We **Nós**	have **temos**	to try to get there **que tentar chegar lá**	You **Tu**	want **queres**	to do him **fazer-lhe**	a lot of good **muito bem**

Lesson 4: Part 3

All You Need To Be Conversant in Portuguese are "<u>The Infinitive Verbs</u>" which are the Foundation of this method.

- <u>The Infinitive Verbs</u> are used the same way and even on the same spot in both Portuguese and English .

- <u>The Infinitive Verbs</u> are never the 1st. Verb on a phrase :

  I   want   to have

  Eu   quero   ter

- <u>The Infinitive Verbs</u> start with "To" in English and End with an "R" in Portuguese:

  To have – **ter**

- <u>The Infinitive Verbs</u> cannot be conjugated:

  ~~I to have~~ – ~~Eu ter~~

- <u>The Infinitive Verbs</u> continue to be used on a phrase endlessly. In this sense the 2 languages are identical.

  I   want   to go to eat

  Eu quero   ir   comer

- The 2nd. <u>Infinitive Verb</u> on a Portuguese Phrase is always Preceded by an "A".

  I   want   to go to sleep

  Eu quero   ir   dormir

- The <u>infinitive Verbs</u> enable through templates to be conversant in four tenses:
  (1) Gerund-action, (2) Past Participle, (3) Future and (4) Conditional.

On the Next Page

You'll find a List of,

Verbos Infinitivos

Infinitive Verbs

Study, Read and Spell them multiple times

'till they stick and……

Notice that all of them (well almost all)

Start with <u>To</u> English

End with <u>R</u> in Portuguese

Lesson 4: Part 4

A

To Accept: aceitar
To Acquire: adquirir
To Allow: permitir
To Announce: anunciar
To Answer: responder
To Argue: discutir
To Approve: aprovar
To Arrive: chegar
To Arrange: organizar
To Ask: perguntar
To Assist: assistir

B

To Be: ser
To Be: ser
To Be Angry: estar zangado
To Be Right: estar certo
To Be Thankful: estar agracedido
To Be Wrong: estar errado
To Become: tornar-se
To Begin: começar
To Believe: acreditar, crer
To Bring: trazer
To Build: construir
To Buy: comprar

C

To Cause: causar
To Call: chamar
Can: poder
To Clean: limpar
To Close: fechar
To Collect: coletar
To Come: vir
To Complete: completar
To Cook: cozinhar
To Copy: copiar
To Correct: corrigir
Could: poderia
To Cry: chorar

D

To Dance: dançar
To Depart: partir
To Discuss: discutir
To Do: fazer
To Doubt: duvidar
To Dress: vestir
To Drink: beber
To Drive: conduzir

E

To Earn: ganhar

To Eat: comer
To Enter: entrar
To Erase: apagar
To Exit: sair

F

To Fall: cair
To Fear: temer
To Feel: sentir
To Find: procurar
To Find Out: descobrir
To Finish: finalizar
To Fit: encaixar
To Follow: seguir
To Forget: esquecer
To Forgive: perdoar

G

To Get: conseguir
To Give: dar
To Go: ir
To Greet: saudar
To Grow: crescer

L

To Laugh: rir
To Learn: aprender
To Leave: sair
To Lend: emprestar
To Listen: ouvir
To Let; deixar
To Like: gostar
To Live: viver
To Look: olhar
To Look (like): parecer

To Lose: perder
To Love: amar
To Live: viver
To Look: olhar
To Look (like): parecer

To Lose: perder
To Love: amar

M

May: maio
To Make: fazer
To Move: mover, mudar
Must: devo

N

To Name: **nomear**
To Need: precisar
To Nix: recusar

O

To Obey: obedecer
To Offer: oferecer
To Observe: observar
To Open: abrir
To Order: pedir
To Owe: dever
To Own: possuir

P

To Pardon: perdoar
To Pay: pagar
To Pick(select): selecionar
To Pick: escolher
To Play (instrument): tocar
To Pull: puxar
To Purchase: comprar
To Push: empurrar
To Put: por

R

To Read: ler
To Realize: perceber
To Refuse: recusar
To Reject: rejeitar
To Remember: lembrar
To Repeat: repetir
To Reply: responder
To Request: pedir
To Respect: respeitar
To Rest: descansar
To Return: voltar
To Run: correr

S

To Save: salvar
To Satisfy: satisfazer
To Say: dizer
To See: ver
To Seek: procurer, buscar
To Sell: vender
To Send: enviar
Shall: deve
Should: deveria
To Show: mostrar
To Shop: comprar
To Sit: sentar

To Sleep: dormir
To Smile: sorrir
To Solve: resolver
To Speak: falar
To Start: começar
To Study: estudar

T

To Take: pegar
To Take: pegar
To Talk: falar
To Teach: ensinar
To Tell: contar
To Terminate: terminar
To Thank: agradecer
To Think: pensar
To Travel: viajar
To Trot: trotar
To Try: tentar

U

To Understand : entender
To Use: usar
To Utilize: utilizar

V

To Value; apreciar
To Visit: visitar

W

To Wait: esperar
To Walk: caminhar
To Want: querer
To Wash: lavar
To Watch: assistir, observar
To Wear: vestir
To Wish: desejar
To Win: ganhar
To Work: trabalhar
To Write: escrever

Y

To Yawn: bocejar

Z

To Zip: fechar

Learning Step 7

The '4' Trigger verbs

enable you to initiate any basic conversation

Practice them, especially the conjugations and the pronunciation

Lessons 5, 6, 7 & 8

**The following 4 "Trigger Verbs"
enable you to initiate most conversations**

Lesson No. 5	Lesson No. 6
To be **Ser, Estar**	To have **Ter**
Lesson No. 7	Lesson No. 8
To want **Querer**	Can **Poder**

Lesson 5: Part 1

The 1st. Trigger Verb is "To Be"
It has two meanings in Portuguese.

Let us first review the verb "**ser**" :
"**ser**" describes a quasi-permanent situation ,
meaning a permanent or an almost permanent situation or condition.

Examples:

I	am	tall		He	is	a policeman
Eu	**sou**	**alto**		**Ele**	**é**	**um policia**
She	is	smart		You	are	single
Ela	**é**	**inteligente**		**Tú**	**és**	**solteiro**
They	are	fanatics		He	is	late
Eles	**são**	**fanáticos**		**Ele**	**está**	**atrasado**
It	is	late		She	is	beautiful
Isto	**é**	**tarde**		**Ela**	**é**	**bonita**

Lesson 5: Part 2

The 1st. Trigger Verb is "To Be"
It has two meanings in Portuguese.

Let us first review the verb "**estar**" :

"**estar**" describes a transitory situation or condition (something passing).

Examples:

I	am	angry	She	is	sick
Eu	**estou**	**zangado**	**Ela**	**está**	**doente**
You	are	late	They	are	ready
Tú	**estás**	**atrasado**	**Eles**	**estão**	**prontos**
He	is	tired	You	are	out
Ele	**está**	**cansado**	**Tu**	**estás**	**fora**
She	is	wrong	It	is	right
Ela	**está**	**errada**	**Isso**	**está**	**certo**

Lesson 5: Part 3

The Trigger Verbs: **To be – ser/estar**

Examples of the verb "ser" (Quasi-permanent situation)	Examples of the verb "estar" (temporary situation)
I am a good player **Eu sou um bom jogador**	I am eating early each day **Estou a comer pronto cada dia**
I am a great person **Eu sou uma boa pessoa**	I am waiting for you now **Estou a tua espera agora**
You are a good man **Tú es um bom homem**	You are tired every day **Tú estas cansada todos os dias**
You are a disgusting person **Tú es uma pessoa nojenta**	You are upset about the game **Tú estas estressada por causa do jogo**
He is an excellent student **Ele é um optimo estudante**	He is taking them to the airport **Ele está a leva-los ao aeroporto**
He is a fantastic cook **Ele é um cozinheiro fantastico**	He is going to visit you this weekend **Ele vai te visitor este fin de semana**
We are always here for you **Nós estamos sempre aqui para ti**	She is coming home for Thanksgiving **Ela esá a vir a casa por Acção de Graças**
You are a winning team **Vocês são a equipe ganhadora**	We are thinking about you **Estamos a pensar em ti**
We are the same people **Nós somos sempre os mesmos**	You are frustrated by the whole situation **Estás frustrado pela situação**
You are never on time **Tú nunca estás a tempo**	They are very tired after the trip **Eles estão muito cansados depois da viajem**
They are the best in town **Eles são os melhores da cidade**	It is getting late **Está a ficar tarde**
They are the worst there is **Eles são os piores que há**	We are doing our homework **Estamos a fazer o teu trabalho de casa**
It is better if you don't come **É melhor se não vieres**	She is trying to finish her task today **Ela está a tentar acabar a sua tarefa hoje**

Lesson 6: Part 1

The 2nd Trigger Verb is "To Have"
It has two meanings in Portuguese:

Let us review first the Verb "**Ter**" in Portuguese.

    "**Ter**" has two meanings in Portuguese:

      1) which describes either ownership/hold/possession or

      2) which denotes duty/responsibility

Examples:

I	have	an automobile	I	have	to go to eat
Eu	**tenho**	**um carro**	**Eu**	**tenho que**	**ir comer**
He	has	an extended family	I	have to	talk with him
Ele	**tem**	**uma extensa familia**	**Eu**	**tenho que**	**falar com ele**
You	have	a problem	He	has to	take you home
Tú	**tens**	**um problema**	**Ele**	**tem que**	**levar-te a casa**
She	has	a headache	We	have	to see you
Ela	**tem**	**dor de cabeça**	**Nós**	**temos que**	**ver-te**
You	have	a visitor	He	has	to live now
Tú	**tens**	**uma visita**	**Ele**	**tem**	**que viver agora**

Lesson 6: Part 2

The 2nd Trigger Verb is "To Have"
It has two meanings in Portuguese:

The Verb "**ter**" in Portuguese is also an auxiliary verb to Past Participle Verbs. Most Past Participle Verbs in Portuguese end in **i or o.**

Examples:

I have gotten mail today **Eu tenho recebido correio hoje**	I have gone to eat **Eu fui comer**
You have taken a long time **Levas-te muito tempo**	You have not called me **Tu não me ligaste**
She has slept in the morning **Ela durmiu de manhã**	He has come to see me **Ele veio me ver**
They have studied all day **Eles estudaram todo o dia**	She has taken me home **Ela levou-me à casa**
They have cooked all morning **Eles têm cozinhado toda a manhã**	I have not gone to sleep **Eu não fui dormir**
He has been running all afternoon **Ele tem corrido toda a tarde**	They have not watched TV **Eles não tem assistido a TV**

Lesson 6: Part 3

Here are examples of the Verb "Ter" in Portuguese,
It is used as an auxiliary verb to speak in Past Participle

To Have: Ter

I have done **Eu tenho feito**	They have studied **Eles tem estudado**	You have understood **Eu tenho percebido**
I have gotten **Eu tenho conseguido**	I have run **Eu tenho corrido**	He has written **Ele tem escrito**
I have taken **Eu tenho tomado**	She has walked **Ela tem caminhado**	I have healed **Eu tenho curado**
You have cooked **Tu tens cozinhado**	They have called **Eles tem chamado**	You have improved **Tu tens melhorado**
He has waited **Ele tem esperado**	I have spoken **Eu tem falado**	They have thought **Eles tem pensado**
She has gone **Ela tem ido**	I have bought it **Eu tenho comprado**	You have brought it **Tu tens comprado**
She has seen **Ela tem visto**	She has shopped **Ela tem comprado**	She has bathed **Ela tem tomado banho**

Lesson 6: Part 3

I have a great family **Eu tenho uma grande familia**	I have to see you tomorrow **Eu tenho que ver-te amanhã**	I have received mail today **Eu tenho recebido correio hoje**
I have a headache **Eu tenho dor de cabeça**	I have to come to see you **Eu vim te ver**	I have slept well yesterday-night **Eu dormí bem ontem a noite**
You have four good kids **Tu tens quatro filhos bons**	You have to go to eat **Tu tens que ir comer**	You have not done your work **Tu não tens feito o teu trabalho**
I have a good job **Eu tenho um bom trabalho**	I have to meet with him today **Eu tenho que encontrar-me com ele hoje**	I have seen her early today **Eu vi-a hoje cedo**
He has problems with her **Ele tem problemas com ela**	He has to bring him the food **Ele tem de lhe trazer a comida**	He has made a big mistake **Ele tem feito um grande erro**
They have a great life **Eles tem uma óptima vida**	They have to hurry up **Ele tem que apressar-se**	They have eaten a lot today **Eles tem comido muito hoje**
You have a lot of luck **Tu tens muita sorte**	You have to finish the project **Tu tens que acabar o projecto**	We have sent her to school **Nos enviamo-la para a escola**
I have a rough road ahead **Eu tenho uma dura estrada a frente**	You have been absent lately **Tu tens estado ausente ultimamente**	We have to start moving **Nos temos que começar a mover**
You have a lot of luck **Tu tens muita sorte**	She has to pay attention **Ela tem que prestar atenção**	She has bought new clothes **Ela comprou roupas novas**
She has a brand new car **Ela tem um carro novo**	It has to be fixed **Isso tem de ser arranjado**	It has been repaired already **Isso já tem sido reparado**
It has a broken light **Tem quebrado luz**	I have to start all over again **Eu tenho de começar de novo**	I have been thinking about it **Eu tenho estado pensando nisso**

Lesson 7: Part 1

**3rd . Trigger Verb "To Want" is used in Portuguese
to Express either Desire or To Give an order:**

Let us now review the Verb **"querer "** in Portuguese, it has two forms:
    1) The Verb **"querer "** in Portuguese is used to express a desire or a wish
    2) The Verb **"querer"** is used to express a command, request or order.

Examples:

	To express a desire	To give an order
I want: **Eu quero** You want: **Tu queres** He wants**: Ele quer** She wants: **Ela quer** We want**: Nos queremos** You want: **Vós quereis** They want: **Eles querem**	I want to go to sleep **Eu quero ir dormir**	I want you to go to eat **Eu quero ir comer**
	I want to learn to sing **Eu quero aprender a cantar**	He wants you to write to him **Ele quer que escrevas-lhe**
	She wants to cook for you **Ela quer cozinhar para ti**	We want you to think about it **Nós queremos que penses sobre isso**
	They want to take you home **Eles querem levar-te à casa**	I want you to bring me the check **Eu quero que me tragas o cheque**

Lesson 7: Part 1

Examples

Desire/ Wish Querer	Command/ Order Querer
I want to take you to the movies **Eu quero te levar ao cinema**	I want that you stop calling me **Eu quero que pares de me ligar**
I want to go shopping today after lunch **Eu quero ir de compras hoje depois do almoço**	I want that you think about it carefully **Eu quero que penses nisso cuidadosamente**
You want me to bring you anything? **Queres que eu te traga qualquer**	Do you want that we get him ready? **Queres que o tenhamos pronto?**
He wants to buy a brand-new pair of shoes **Ele quer comprar um par de sapatos novos**	He wants that you call him today at 2 p.m. **Ele quer que o chames hoje as 2 pm**
She wants to try to find a new job **Ela quer tentar encontrar um trabalho novo**	She wants me not to bother her anymore **Ela quer que eu não a incommode mais**

Lesson 8: Part 1

The 4th Trigger Verb "Can" is used in Portuguese to express "Being Able To".

In Portuguese can means "Poder".

Examples:

I can see you later **Eu posso ver-te mais logo**	He can come at noon **Ele pode vir ao meio dia**
She can go to see him **Ela pode ir o ver**	You can do it **Tu o podes fazer**
They can take you home **Eles te podem levar à casa**	You can come in **Tu podes entrar**
He can come tomorrow **Ele pode vir amanhã**	I can call you later **Eu posso te ligar logo**

Lesson 8: Part 2

Examples:

I can come to see you this weekend **Eu posso vir te ver esse fim de semana**	He can prepare for the test this week **Ele pode preparar para a prova essa semana**
I can call you every night at 8 p.m. **Eu posso ligar-te todas as noites às 20 horas**	You can bring them over to spend the day here **Tu podes trazê-los para passar o dia aqui**
He can take them to the park tomorrow at 4 **Ele pode leva-las ao parque amanhã às 14 horas**	You can go to the movies with them **Tu podes ir ao cinema com eles**
She can not eat chicken **Ela não pode comer frango**	You can call me after lunch **Tu podes ligar-me depois do almoço**
We can work together to solve the problem **Nós podemos trabalhar juntos para resolver o problema**	They can complain all they want, it won't make a difference **Eles podem se queixar quanto eles quiserem, não vai fazer diferença nenhuma**

Lesson 9: Part 1

Ok. Let's use the Nouns, The 4 Trigger Verbs, The Magic Words and additional Infinitive Verbs to build more phrases.

I – Eu You – Tu He – Ele She – Ela We – Nós You – Vós They – Eles, Elas It – Isso	**I have to go to call her** Eu tenho de a chamar	**I want to come to see you** Eu quero vir te ver
	I want to take you to dinner Eu quero te levar a jantar	**You can go to sleep** Tu podes ir dormir
	He can wait for you at noon Ele pode esperar por ti ao meio dia	**She wants to cook for you** Ela quer cozinhar para ti
	I have to go to take notes Eu tenho de ir tomar nota	**I have to run to go to see him** Eu tenho de ir correndo lhe ver
The 4 Trigger Verbs To Be – Ser/ Estar To Have – Ter To Have – Haver To Want – Querer Can – Poder	**I can go to see you tomorrow** Eu posso ir ver-te amanhã	**They can come to run tonight** Eles podem vir corer à noite
	We can cook rather quickly Nós podemos cozinhar rápido	**He has to call her soon** Ele tem que chamar ela pronto
	We have to wait for her Nós temos que esperar por ela	

Lesson 9: Part 2

Additional Trigger Verbs	
To go	**Ir**
To come	**Vir**
To take	**Levar**
To buy	**Comprar**
To cook	**Cozinhar**
To wait	**Esperar**
To run	**Correr**
To watch	**Observar**
To see	**Ver**
To give	**Dar**
To get	**Receber**
To walk	**Caminhar**
To write	**Escrever**

Examples

You have to come to see her **Tu tens de vir e vê-la**	He has to get mail this week **Ele tem de procurar correio esta semana**
You can come to watch TV later **Tu podes vir e assistir TV mais tarde**	He has to go to get his ID **Ele tem que buscar o seu cartão de identificação.**
She wants you to call soon **Ela quer que a ligues pronto**	He has to learn to write often **Ele tem de aprender a escrever frequentemente**
He can read pretty well **Ele pode ler muito bem**	They have to run today **Eles têm de correr hoje**
She wants to run every morning **Ela quer correr todas as manhãs**	They can take you to the airport now **Eles querem levar-te agora para o aeroporto**
You can go to buy groceries at three **Tu podes ir às compras de mercearia às três em ponto**	

Lesson 9: Part 3

Now, "Let's" build phrases with what we have learned

I have to be a good father **Eu tenho de ser um bom pai**	I have to be there on time **Eu tenho de ser pontual**	He has to be patient **Ele tem de ser paciente**
I want to be fair **Eu tenho de ser justo**	I want to be present **Eu quero estar presente**	He wants to be like his father **Ele quer ser como o seu pai**
I can be often late **Eu posso chegar tarde com frequência**	I can be there at two **Eu quero estar lá às duas da tarde**	He can be a very good team mate **Ele pode ser um bom companheiro de equipa**
You have to be persistent **Tu tens de ser persistente**	You can have a lot of trouble soon **Tu podes meter-te em muitos problemas em breve**	We want to be ready for him **Nós queremos estar prontos para ele**
You want to be the best **Tu tens de ser o melhor**	You want to be ahead of the curve **Tu queres estar em frente dos outros**	We can be in the losing end **Nós podemos estar do lado perdedor**
You can be the last to come in **Tu podes ser o último a chega**	You have to be alert all the time **Tu tens de estar sempre alerta**	He has to be devastated **Ele tem de ser devastado**
We have to be polite **Nós temos de ser educados**	We have to be waiting for him at the gate **Nós temos de esperar por ele à porta**	He wants to be permanently on vacations **Ele quer estar sempre de férias**
We want to be the best **Nós queremos ser os melhores**	He can be available later **Ele pode estar disponível mais tarde**	We can be of great help to you **Nós podemos ajudar-te**

Lesson 9: Part 4

The Infinitive Verbs/ The Four Trigger Verbs

Nouns	To Be **Ser**	To Want **Quer**	To Have **Ter**	Can **Poder**	Will **Ir**
I/ **Eu**	sou	quero	tenho	posso	vou
You/ **Tu**	es	queres	tens	podes	vais
He/ **Ele**	é	quer	tem	pode	vai
She/ **Ela**	é	quer	tem	pode	vai
We/ **Nós**	somos	queremos	temos	podemos	vamos
You / **Vós**	sois	quereis	tendes	podeis	ides
They/ **Eles/Elas**	são	querem	têm	podem	vão
It/ **Isso**					

Learning Step 8

The 4 Templates

Enable you to be conversant in:

➢ Gerund (action)

➢ Past Participle

➢ Future

➢ Conditional tenses

while using only "Infinitive Verbs"

Gerundio/ Gerund (Action)

ENGLISH: To Be + a Verb that ends in "ing"
PORTUGUESE: **Ser, estar** + a Verb that ends in either "ando", "endo" or "indo"

How to convert a Portuguese "Infinitive Verb" into "Gerund" (Action):

Example 1:
To Walk — Kill the "To"— add "ing" Walking
anda<u>r</u> — Kill the "R"— then add "ando" **and<u>ando</u>**

<u>I am walking to eat</u>
Estou and<u>ando</u> para comer

Example 2:
To Run — Kill the "To" — add "ing" Running
corre<u>r</u> — Kill the "R"— then add "endo" **corr<u>endo</u>**

<u>I am running every morning</u>
Estou corr<u>endo</u> todas as manhãs

Example 3:
To Sleep — Kill "To" — add "ing" Sleeping
dormi<u>r</u> — Kill "R"— then add "indo" **dorm<u>indo</u>**

<u>I am sleeping now</u>
Eu estou dorm<u>indo</u> agora

Lesson 10: Part 1

ENGLISH : To Be + Verb ending in **"ing"**
PORTUGUESE : **ser, estar** + Verb ending in "ando" "endo" or "indo"

➢ In English we speak in Gerund when we refer to "Action."
➢ And we use the Verb "To Be" followed followed by a verb ending in ing.
➢ In Portuguese is exactly the same,

Example:
To Call: I am calling you tonight
Chamar   **chamando**
So, bottom line: verb endings in ing in English end in either "ando" "endo" or "indo"

How to convert an Infinitive Verb to Gerund:

In English we do this:
To Call----Calling (kill the "To" then add "ing")

In Portuguese they do this:
Chamar----Chamando (kill the "r" then add "ando")

Lesson 10: Part 2

Examples

I am calling you now **Eu estou chamando-te agora**	They are calling him today **Eles estão chamando-le hoje**	They are calling tonight **Eles estão chamando hoje**
I am studying all morning **Estou estudando toda a manhã**	They are studying today **Eles estão estudando hoje**	She is studying now **Ela está estudando agora**
I am waiting at the house **Estou esperando em casa**	We are waiting for you **Estamos esperando por ti**	You are waiting in vain **Tu estás esperando em vão**
I am writing to you every week **Estou escrevendo-te todas as semanas**	They are writing every other week **Eles estão escrevendo todas as semanas**	He is writing often **Ele está escrevendo frequentemente**
I am trying to visit you **Estou tentando visitar-te**	She is trying to visit us **Ela está tentando visitar-nos**	They are trying to call **Eles estão tentando chamar**
I am learning to speak **Estou aprendendo a falar**	She is learning about the country **Ela está aprendendo sobre o condado**	He is learning the basic **Ele está aprendendo o básico**
I am watching hispanic TV **Estou assistindo televisão hispânica**	You are watching her grow **Tu estas vendo ela crescer**	He is watching the game **Ele está vendo o jogo**

Infinitive Verbs:

To Call : chamar   To Study : estudar   To Wait : esperar   To Write: escrever

To Try: tentar   To Learn: aprender   To Watch: ver

Participle/Participio (Past Participle)

ENGLISH: To Have + Past Participle Verb
PORTUGUESE: **Ter** + a verb that ends in either "ido", "indo" or "ado"

How to convert a Portuguese "Infinitive Verb" into "Gerund" (Action):

Example 1:
To Wal<u>r</u> — **andar** — Kill the "R"— then add "ado" **and<u>ado</u>**

<u>I have walked all morning</u>
Eu tenho camin<u>ado</u> tuda a mañana

Example 2:
To Run — **corre<u>r</u>** — Kill the "R"— then add "ido" **corr<u>ido</u>**

<u>I have run yesterday night</u>
Eu tenho corr<u>ido</u> ontem à noite

Example 3:
To Sleep — **dormir** — Kill "R"— then add "ido" Walking **dormido**

<u>I have slept all morning</u>
Eu tenho dorm<u>ido</u> tuda a mañana

Examples

To take: I have taken her home **Levar: Eu tenho levado-a para casa**	To wait: They have been waiting for you **Esperar: Eles têm estado à tua espera**
To eat: He has eaten at 12 **Comer: Ele têm comido às 12 horas**	To wash: She has been washing all morning **Lavar: Ela têm estado a lavar toda a manhã**
To learn: They have learned to read **Aprender: Eles têm aprendido a ler**	To ask: He has been asking for you **Perguntar: Ele tem estado a perguntar por ti**
To talk: She has talked to him **Falar: Ela têm falado com ele**	To cook: They have been cooking today **Cozinhar: Eles têm estado a cozinhar hoje**
To study: We have studied all day **Estudar: Nós temos estudiado o dia todo**	To walk: We have walked **Caminhar: Nós temos caminhado**
To get: They have gotten no mail **Receber: Eles não têm recebido um email**	To think: You have thought about it **Pensar: Tu tens pensado sobre isso**
To go: I have gone to see her **Ir: Eu têm ido a vê-la**	To come: You have been coming every year **Ver: Tu tens vindo todos os anos**
To bring: He has brought a friend **Trazer: Ele têm trazido um amigo**	To win: We have been winning more **Ganhar: Nós temos estado ganhando mais**
To listen: She has listened to him **Ouvir : Ela têm estado a ouvir o que ele diz**	To buy: I have been buying lots of vitamins **Comprar: Eu tenho estado comprando muitas vitaminas**

Past Participle (Verbs)/ (Verbos) Pasado Participio

Been	Been	Arrived	Washed	Cooled	Packed	Written	Fought
Sendo	**Estando**	**Chegou**	**Lavado**	**Resfriado**	**Embalado**	**Escrito**	**Lutado**
Come	Talked	Calculated	Explained	Looked	Brought	Replied	Thought
Vir	**Falado**	**Calculado**	**Explicado**	**Olhado**	**Trazido**	**Respondido**	**Pensado**
Gotten	Taken	Seen	Repeated	Appealed	Needed	Heated	Watched
Conseguido	**Levado**	**Visto**	**Repetido**	**Apelado**	**Necessitado**	**Aquecido**	**Visto**
Ran	Cleaned	Called	Had	Finished	Disputed	Cooked	Replied
Corrido	**Limpado**	**Chamado**	**Teve**	**Finalizado**	**Disputado**	**Cozinhado**	**Respondido**
Done	Failed	Given	Listened	Accepted	Built	Traveled	Grabbed
Feito	**Falhado**	**Dado**	**Ouvido**	**Aceitei**	**Construido**	**Viajado**	**Pegado**
Wished	Made	Walked	Bought	Asked	Wanted	Realized	Started
Desejado	**Feito**	**Caminhado**	**Comprado**	**Perguntado**	**Querido**	**Realizado**	**Começado**
Remembered	Baked	Put	Sat	Read	Eaten	Gone	Enjoyed
Lembrado	**Assado**	**Colocado**	**Sentado**	**Lido**	**Comido**	**Ido**	**Apreciado**
Fried	Heard	Lost	Liked	Stood	Bathed	Said	Searched
Frito	**Escutado**	**Perdido**	**Gostado**	**Parado**	**Banhado**	**Disse**	**Pesquisado**
Slept	Agreed	Exited	Left	Loved	Woken	Layed	Saddened
Dormido	**Concordado**	**Existido**	**Deixado**	**Amado**	**Acordado**	**Deitado**	**Entristecido**
Questioned	Entered	Hurt	Found	Flown	Won	Cried	Shipped
Questionado	**Entrado**	**Ferido**	**Encontrado**	**Voado**	**Ganhado**	**Chorado**	**Expedido**
Ordered	Boiled	Dreamed	Drank	Paid	Swam	Waited	Started
Encomendado	**Cozido**	**Sonhado**	**Bebido**	**Pago**	**Nadado**	**Esperado**	**Começado**
Answered	Understood	Argued	Jumped	Forgotten	Discussed	Dried	Shown
Respondido	**Entendido**	**Discutido**	**Saltado**	**Esquecido**	**Debatido**	**Secado**	**Mostrado**

Future/ Futuro

ENGLISH: Will + Infinitive Verb.
PORTUGUESE: ir + Infinitive Verb.

I will = **irei**
You will = **irás**
He will = **irá**
She will = **irá**
We will = **iremos**
You Will = **ireis**
They will = **irão**

Example:

To go = Ir   To eat = Comer

<u>I   will go   to eat   later</u>
Eu   vou ir   comer   mais tarde

Lesson 12: Part 1

Examples

I will go to run later **Eu vou ir correr mais tarde**	They will go to visit you soon **Eles irão visitar-te em breve**
You will not finish **Tu não irás a terminar**	I will study all day **Eu irei estudar o dia todo**
She will call you later **Ela irá chamar-te mais tarde**	They will get your food **Eles irão trazer-te a tua comida**
You will take me home **Tu irás levar-me para casa**	He will cook for you today **Eles irão cozinhar para ti hoje**
He will wait for you at 12 **Ele irá esperar por ti às 12 horas**	He will fly out at 3 **Ele irá voar às 3**
He will bring you lunch at 1 **Ele irá trazer-te o almoço à 1**	You will not be on time **Não irás conseguir chegar a tempo**

Conditional/ Condicional

What is a conditional verb?

Any verb that depicts a condition ;

In English any verb that ends in "ould",

In Portuguese any verb that ends in "iria",

How to convert a Portuguese Verb into a Conditional tense Verb?

ENGLISH: Could
               Should   } + Infinitive verb
               Would

PORTUGUESE: Add "ia" to any Infinitive verb

Example:

To go = **iria**   To run = **correria**

I would go to run if you would come with me

Eu iria corer se viéreis comigo

Lesson 13: Part 1

Examples

He'd try to finish tomorrow if he gets paid **Ele poderia tentar terminar amanhã se lhe pagarem**	
I could go to run if the weather is nice **Eu poderia ir correr se o tempo estivesse bom**	
You should come to study only if you are ready for it **Tu só devias vir para estudar se estiveres preparado para isso**	
I would go to visit you if you would be available for me **Eu deveria vir visitar-te se estiveres disponível para mim**	
We would eat at your place if you would cook for all of us **Nós deveríamos comer em tua casa se cozinhas para todos**	
They would call you at noon if you could have an answer for them **Eles deveriam ligar-te ao meio-dia, se tiveres uma resposta para eles**	
I would take you to the airport if you are ready by 8 **Eu deveria levar-te ao aeroporto se estiveres pronto às 8 horas**	
You would be very happy if you could just try to lend a hand **Tu deverias estar muito feliz se eu apenas tentasse ajudar-te**	
She would wait for them at noon if they are all showing up **Ela deveria esperar por eles ao meio-dia, se todos aparecerem**	
They would prefer if you don't do anything for the moment **Eles preferem que você não faça nada no momento**	

Infinitive Verbs

Can	**Poder**
Shall	**Dever**
To go	**Ir**
To eat	**Comer**
To call	**Ligar**
To wait	**Esperar**
To talk	**Falar**
To study	**Estudar**
To buy	**Comprar**
To take	**Tomar**

Conditional Verbs

Could	**Poderia**
Should	**Deveria**
Would eat	**Comeria**
Would call	**Ligaria**
Would wait	**Esperaria**
Would talk	**Falaria**
Would study	**Estudaria**
Would buy	**Compraria**
Would take	**Tomaria**

The Four Templates

Through this method you'll build any phrase with an "Infinitive Verb"
Using the same verbs, let us build some sentences using the four templates.

Gerund/ Gerundio (Action)	**Participle/Participio**
To eat = **comendo**	To eat = **comido**
I am eating = **estou comendo**	I have eaten = **tenho comido**
To walk = **caminhando**	To walk = **caminhado**
He is walking = **ele está caminhando**	He has walked = **ele tem caminhado**
Future/ Futuro	**Conditional/Condicional**
To eat = **comerei**	To Eat = **comeria**
I will eat = **Eu vou ir comer**	I would eat = **Eu iria comer**
To walk = **caminharei**	To Walk = **caminharia**
He will walk = **Ele vai ir caminhar**	He would walk = **Eu iria caminhar**

Learning Step 9

The 11 Verbs

We revisit English grammar in order to translate properly from English to Portuguese

Pay close attention to these 11 verbs because you need proper English to speak proper Portuguese!

Lesson 14

To be	**Ser, estar**	To have	**Ter**	Can	**Poder**
Could	**Poder**	Shall	**Dever**	Should	**Dever**
Will	**Ir**	Must	**Tenher**	Might	**Poder**
May	**Dever**	Would	**Poder**		

These verbs have unique features that we need to be mindful of:

1) If any other verb follows one of these 11 verbs, there is never a "To" after it.
Examples : In English most of the times a "To" follows a 1st. verb: I have to go – I want to go – I like to go. Not on these 11 verbs: I am going – I can go – I could go – I may go – I will go.

2) Except for the verbs To Be & To Have the infinitive form of the other 9 verbs is w/o a "To."
Example : Can, May, Shall always start w/o a "To".

3) When asking a question with these 11 verbs, we don't use "Do" or "Did" at the beginning of the question; simply flip the verb & the noun (which is the only way Hispanics do it).
Example : Normally is: Do I want?-Did I have?, But with these 11 verbs we just flip":Am I?-Can I?

4) When Negating with these 11 verbs, we don't use "Don't" or "Didn't" we simply add "not" after the verb.
Example : Normally is: I don't want – I don't have to. But with these Verbs we negate as follows: I am not coming, You can not go, You have not eaten.

5) Except for To Be & To Have, these verbs have no conjugations
Example : I can-He can / I may- He may / we must-they must

Learning Step 10

Questions & Negations

As you'll see both questions and negations are far easier in Portuguese than in English.

Lesson 15

Questions

In Portuguese, Questions are formulated by ending the sentence on a question mark tone?

Examples:

Do you want to go to eat?
Tu queres ir almoçar?

Do you have to come?
Tu tens de vir?

Can I go to visit her?
Eu posso ir visitá-la?

Should she call me?
Ela deveria ligar-me?

Negations

In Portuguese, Negations are always and only formulated by inserting a Não (Nahoh) right after the noun.

Examples:

You do not want to go to eat
Tu não queres ir almoçar

You don´t have to come
Tu não tens de vir

I can not go to visit her
Eu não posso ir visitá-la

She should not call me
Ela não deveria ligar-me

Learning Step 11

"There is"

These two words are expressed in Portuguese through one word:

"HAY" (AHEE)

Lesson 16

There is

There is: **Há**

There are: **Há**

There was: **Havia**

There were: **Havia**

There has been: **Houve**

There have been: **Houve**

There will be: **Haverá**

There would be: **Haveria**

There would have been: **Haveria**

Learning Step 12

"Er-Est-Y"

Learn how these endings are expressed in Portuguese

Practice them, especially the conjugations!

The Endings Er - Est - Y

Better	Melhor
Taller	Mais Alto
Faster	Mais Rápido
Quicker	Mais Veloz
Smaller	Mais Pequeno
Slower	Mais Lento
Hotter	Mais Quente
Colder	Mais Frio
Dumber	Mais Tonto
Fewer	Menor
Shorty	Baixinho
Tardy	Tardioso
Weepy	Choroso

Best	Melhor
Tallest	Mais Alto
Afastest	Mais Rápido
Quickest	Mais Veloz
Smallest	Mais Pequeno
Slowest	Mais Lento
Hottest	Mais Quente
Coldest	Mais Frio
Dumbest	Mais Tonto
Fewest	Menor
As … As	Curto/Baixo
More … Than	Mais… Que

Examples:

Shorter than
Mais baixo que

Better than
Melhor que

Taller than
Mais Alto que

Faster than
Mais Rápido que

Lesson 17: Part 2

When the ending 'or' is applied to an infinitive verb,
it converts it into a person.

To Drive = **Conduzir**	Driver = **Condutor**
To Eat = **Comer**	Eater = **Comedor**
To Play = **Jogar**	Player = **Jogador**
To Run = **Corrrer**	Runner = **Corredor**
To Sleep = **Dormir**	Sleeper = **Dormidor**
To Write = **Escrever**	Writer = **Escretor**
To Read = **Ler**	Reader = **Leitor**
To Pay = **Pagar**	Payer = **Pagador**
To Wash = **Lavar**	Washer = **Lavador**
To Speak = **Falar**	Speaker = **Falador**

Learning Step 13

The Verb

To Have

Learn the different grammar rules that apply to it

Practice them, especially the pronunciations!

Lesson 18

Uses of the Verb To Have: **Ter**

Hold/ Ownership	Duty/ Responsibility	Past Participle
Examples:	*Examples*:	*Examples*:
I have a headache **Eu tenho dor de cabeça**	I have to go **Eu tenho que ir**	I have done it! **Tenho-o feito!**
I have a son **Eu tenho um filho**	You have to come **Tú tens que vir**	I have gone to eat early **Eu tenho ido comer cedo**
I have a family **Eu tenho uma familia**	I have to go eat **Eu tenho que ir comer**	

Learning Step 14

The Verb

To Like

Learn the different grammar rules that apply to it

Practice them, especially the pronunciations!

Lesson 19

What will happen? **O que é que irá acontecer?**	What happens to you? **O que te vai acontecer?**	It happens to me **O que é que me vai acontecer**
What will you bring? **O que é que irás trazer?**	What would happen to you if **O que aconteceria se**	It would happen to me **isso me acontecesse**
Who will bring you? **Quem te irá trazer?**	What has happened to you? **O que te aconteceu?**	It has happened to me **Isto já me aconteceu**
Who will pick you up? **Quem te irá buscar?**	What will happen to you? **O que é que te irá acontecer?**	It will happen to me **Irá me acontecer**
Who will find you? **Quem te irá encontrar?**	What has been happening to you? **O que aconteceu contigo?**	It has been happening to me **Tem-me estado a acontecer**
Who will cut your hair? **Quem te irá cortar o cabelo?**	Who will wash your car? **A quem irá lavar o teu carro**	I have a headache **Eu Estou com dor de cabeça**
It seems too much for me **Parece-me demasiado para mim**	Bring me back **Leva-me de volta**	My wife takes me **A minha mulher leva-me**
Buy me a pair of shoes **Compra-me um par de sapatos**	I will like a cup of wine **Eu quero um copo de vinho**	You've failed me **Tu falhaste-me**
It does not get through my head **Isso não me passa pela cabeça**	I've lost my car **Eu perdi o meu carro**	I've lost my purse **Eu perdi a minha carteira**
I forgot to call you **Eu esqueci-me de te chamar**	I do not like them at all **Eu não gosto nada deles**	She does not talk to me **Ela não fala comigo**

Lesson 20

List of Verbs conjugated in 3rd Person

Seems **Parece**	Kills **Mata**	Manipulates **Manipula**	Traumatizes **Traumatiza**	Takes **Leva**	Affects **Afecta**
Born **Nasce**	Convinces **Convence**	Fails **Falha**	Loses Control **Perde o Controle**	Attracts **Atrai**	Makes **Cria**
Fits **Encaixa**	Delay **Atrasa**	Fascinates **Fascina**	Finishes **Termina**	Takes **Toma**	Intimidates **Intimida**
Suffices **Basta**	Loses **Pierda**	Talks **Fala**	Gets/Arrives **Recebe/Cjega**	Stops **Para**	Enchants **Encanta**
Worries **Inquieta**	Detains **Pára**	Sympathizes **Simpatiza**	Happens **Acontece**	Worries **Inquieta**	Pains **Dói**
Relaxes **Relaxa**	Intrigues **Intriga**	Falls **Cai**	Enervates **Enerva**	Marvels **Maravilha**	Brings **Traz**
Tires **Cansa**	Causes **Causa**	Skeeds **Patina**	Washes **Lava**	Bores **Aborrece**	Irritates **Irrita**
Wins **Ganha**	Knows **Conhece**	Forgets **Esquece**	Invites **Invita**	Wins **Ganha**	Sleeps **Dorme**
Make Happy **Faz Feliz**	Mortifies **Mortifica**	Motivates **Motiva**	Embarrasses **Envergonha**	Costs **Custa**	Cuts **Corta**
Stuns **Atorda**	Surprises **Surprende**	Scares **Assusta**	Motivates **Motiva**	Entertains **Diverte**	Anguish **Angústia**
Honors **Honra**	Satiates **Sacia**	Illusions **Iusiona**	Prides **Enorgulhese**	Kills **Mata**	Skates **Patina**

Learning Step 15

The Expression

"Just" acabei

(just done/just finished/just completed "it")

Lesson 21

English		Portuguese	
I have just	+ past participle verb	**Acabei de**	+ infinitive verb
You have just	+ past participle verb	**Acabaste de**	+ infinitive verb
He has just	+ past participle verb	**Acabou de**	+ infinitive verb
She has just	+ past participle verb	**Acabou de**	+ infinitive verb
We have just	+ past participle verb	**Acabamos de**	+ infinitive verb
You have just	+ past participle verb	**Acabaste de**	+ infinitive verb
They have just	+ past participle verb	**Acabaram de**	+ infinitive verb
It has just	+ past participle verb	**Acabou de**	+ infinitive verb

Examples:

I have just eaten
Acabei de comer
I have just woken up
Acabei de acordar
He has just phoned us
Ele acabou de chamar-nos
They have just come back from shopping
Eles acabaram de voltar de fazer a compra
You have just committed (made) an error
Acabas de fazer um erro

You have just finished your shift
Acabas de finalizar o teu turno
We have just left
Acabamos de sair
She has just taken him to school
Ela acaba de o levar à escola
I have just remembered the appointment
Acabei de lembrar-me do encontro
You have just missed the movie
Acabas de perder o filme

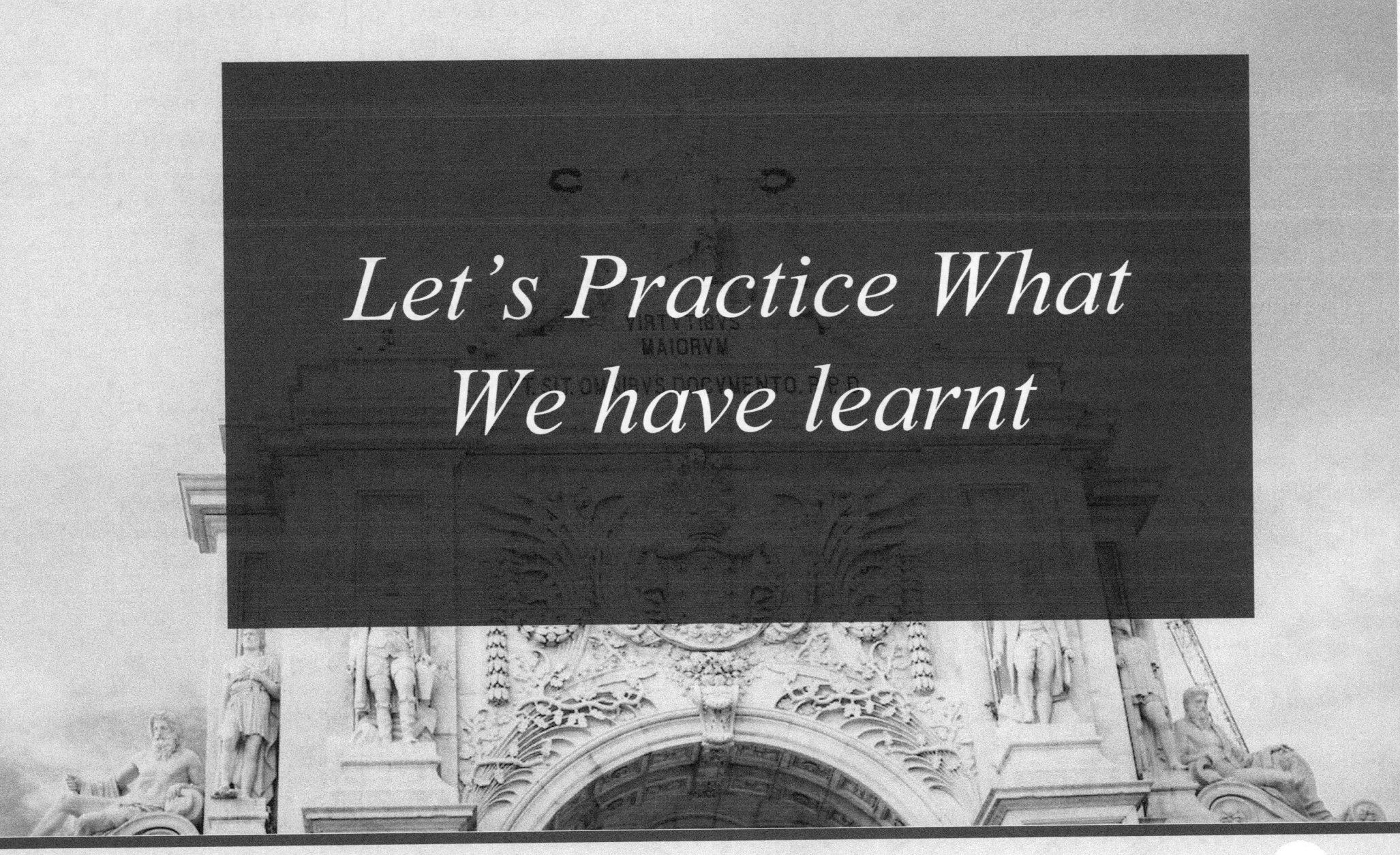

Let's Practice What We have learnt

Infinitives

Example: <u>To Cook / Cozinhar</u> (Infinitive Verb)

Present I cook Eu cozinho	Gerund I am cooking Eu estou cozinhando	Future I will cook Eu irei cozinhar	Past Participle I have cooked Eu já cozinhei	Conditional I would cook Eu cozinharia
I will be cooking Eu estarei cozinhando	I was cooking Eu estava cozinhando	I have to cook Eu tenho que cozinhar	I have been cooking Eu tenho estado cozinhando	
I would have cooked Eu teria cozinhado	I did cook Eu cozinhei			

Example: <u>To Wait / Esperar</u> (Infinitive Verb)

Present I wait Eu espero	Gerund I am waiting Eu estou esperando	Future I will wait Eu irei esperar	Past Participle I have waited Eu tenho esperado	Conditional I would wait Eu esperaria
I will be waiting Eu vou estar esperando	I was waiting Eu estava esperando	I have to wait Eu tenho que esperar	I have been waiting Eu tenho estado esperando	
I would have waited Eu teria esperado	I did wait Eu esperei			

Infinitives

Example: <u>To Run / Correr</u> (Infinitive Verb) The Four Templates

Present	Gerund	Future	Past Participle	Conditional
I run **Eu corro**	I am running **Eu estou correndo**	I will run **Eu irei correr**	I have run **Eu já correi**	I would run **Eu corraria**
I will be running **Eu estarei correndo**	I was running **Eu estava correndo**	I have to run **Eu tenho que correr**	I have been running **Eu tenho estado correndo**	
I would have run **Eu teria corrido**	I ran **Eu corri**			

Example: <u>To Eat / Comer</u> (Infinitive Verb) The Four Templates

Present	Gerund	Future	Past Participle	Conditional
I eat **Eu como**	I am eating **Eu estou comendo**	I will eat **Eu irei comer**	I have eaten **Eu já comi**	I would eat **Eu comeria**
I will be eating **Eu estarei comendo**	I was eating **Eu estava comando**	I have to eat **Eu tenho que comer**	I have been eating **Eu tenho estado comendo**	
I would have eaten **Eu teria comido**	I ate **Eu comi**			

Infinitives

Example: <u>To Talk / Falar</u> (Infinitive Verb)

Present	Gerund	Future	Past Participle	Conditional
I talk	I am talking	I will talk	I have talked	I would talk
Eu falo	**Eu estou falando**	**Eu irei falar**	**Eu já falei**	**Eu falaria**

I will be talking	I was talking	I have to talk	I have been talking
Eu estarei falando	**Eu estava falando**	**Eu tenho que falar**	**Eu tenho estado falando**

I would have spoken	I spoke
Eu teria falado	**Eu falei**

Example: <u>To Call / Chamar</u> (Infinitive Verb)

Present	Gerund	Future	Past Participle	Conditional
I call	I am calling	I will call	I have called	I would call
Eu chamo	**Eu estou chamando**	**Eu irei chamar**	**Eu já chamei**	**Eu chamaria**

I will be calling	I was calling	I have to call	I have been calling
Eu estarei chamando	**Eu estava chamando**	**Eu tenho que chamar**	**Eu tenho estado chamando**

I would have called	I called
Eu teria chamado	**Eu chamei**

Infinitives

The Four Templates

Example: <u>To Take / Levar</u> (Infinitive Verb)

Present	Gerund	Future	Past Participle	Conditional
I take **Eu levo**	I am taking **Eu estou levando**	I will take **Eu irei levar**	I have taken **Eu já levei**	I would take **Eu levaria**
I will be taking **Eu estarei levando**	I was taking **Eu estava levando**	I have to take **Eu tenho que levar**	I have been taking **Eu tenho estado levando**	
I would have taken **Eu teria levado**	I took **Eu levei**			

The Four Templates

Example: <u>To Get / Receber</u> (Infinitive Verb)

Present	Gerund	Future	Past Participle	Conditional
I get **Eu recebo**	I am getting **Eu estou recebendo**	I will get **Eu irei receber**	I have gotten **Eu já recebi**	I would get **Eu receberia**
I will be getting **Eu estarei recebendo**	I was getting **Eu estava recebendo**	I have to get **Eu tenho que receber**	I have been getting **Eu tenho estado recebendo**	
I would have gotten **Eu teria recebido**	I got **Eu recebi**			

Infinitives

Example: <u>To Think / Pensar</u> (Infinitive Verb)

The Four Templates

Present	Gerund	Future	Past Participle	Conditional
I think **Eu penso**	I am thinking **Eu estou pensando**	I will think **Eu irei pensar**	I have thought **Eu já pensei**	I would think **Eu pensaria**
I will be thinking **Eu estarei pensando**	I was thinking **Eu estaba pensando**	I have to think **Eu tenho que pensar**	I have been thinking **Eu tenho estado pensando**	
I would have thought **Eu teria pensado**	I thought **Eu pensei**			

Example: <u>To Study / Estudar</u> (Infinitive Verb)

The Four Templates

Present	Gerund	Future	Past Participle	Conditional
I study **Eu estudo**	I am studying **Eu estou estudando**	I will study **Eu irei estudar**	I have studied **Eu já estudei**	I would study **Eu estudaria**
I will be studying **Eu estarei estudando**	I was studying **Eu estava estudando**	I have to study **Eu tenho que estudar**	I have been studyting **Eu tenho estado estudando**	
I would have studied **Eu teria estudado**	I studied **Eu estudei**			

Infinitives

Example: To Write / Escrever (Infinitive Verb)

Present I write **Eu escrevo**	Gerund I am writing **Eu estou escrevendo**	Future I will write **Eu irei escrevar**	Past Participle I have written **Eu já escrevi**	Conditional I would write **Eu escreveria**
I will be writing **Eu estarei escrevendo**	I was writing **Eu estaba escrevendo**	I have to write **Eu tenho que escrever**		I have been writing **Eu tenho estado escrevendo**
I would have wrote **Eu teria escrito**	I wrote **Eu escrevei**			

Example: To Read / Ler (Infinitive Verb)

The Four Templates

Present I read **Eu leio**	Gerund I am reading **Eu estou lendo**	Future I will read **Eu irei ler**	Past Participle I have read **Eu tenho lido**	Conditional I would read **Eu leria**
I will be reading **Eu estarei lendo**	I was reading **Eu estava lendo**	I have to read **Eu tenho que ler**		I have been reading **Eu tenho estado lendo**
I would have read **Eu teria lido**	I read **Eu leio**			

Infinitives

Example: <u>To Do / Fazer</u> (Infinitive Verb)

The Four Templates

Present I do **Eu faço**	Gerund I am doing **Eu estou fazendo**	Future I will do **Eu irei fazar**	Past Participle I have done **Eu já fiz**	Conditional I would do **Eu faria**
I will be doing **Eu estarei fazendo**	I was doing **Eu estaba fazendo**	I have to do **Eu tenho que fazer**		I have been doing **Eu tenho estado fazendo**
I would have done **Eu teria feito**	I did **Eu fiz**			

Example: <u>To Work / Trabalhar</u> (Infinitive Verb)

The Four Templates

Present I work **Eu trabalho**	Gerund I am working **Eu estou trabalhando**	Future I will work **Eu irei trabalhar**	Past Participle I have worked **Eu já trabalhado**	Conditional I would work **Eu trabalharia**
I will be working **Eu estarei trabalhando**	I was working **Eu estava trabalhando**	I have to work **Eu tenho que trabalhar**		I have been working **Eu tenho estado trabalhando**
I would have worked **Eu teria trabalhado**	I worked **Eu trabalhei**			

Negation

Example: <u>To Cook / Cozinhar</u> (Infinitive Verb)

Present I don't cook **Eu não cozinho**	Gerund I am not cooking **Eu não estou cozinhando**	Future I won't cook **Eu não irei cozinhar**	Past Participle I haven't cooked **Eu não já cozinhei**	Conditional I wouldn't cook **Eu não cozinharia**
I won't be cooking **Eu não estarei cozinhando**	I wasn't cooking **Eu não estava cozinhando**	I don't have to cook **Eu não tenho que cozinhar**	I haven't been cooking **Eu não tenho estado cozinhando**	
I wouldn't have cooked **Eu não teria cozinhado**	I didn't cook **Eu não cozinhei**			

Example: <u>To Wait / Esperar</u> (Infinitive Verb)

Present I don't wait **Eu não espero**	Gerund I am not waiting **Eu não estou esperando**	Future I won't wait **Eu não irei esperar**	Past Participle I haven't waited **Eu não tenho esperado**	Conditional I wouldn't wait **Eu não esperaria**
I won't be waiting **Eu não estar esperando**	I wasn't waiting **Eu não estava esperando**	I don't have to wait **Eu não tenho que esperar**	I haven't been waiting **Eu não tenho estado esperando**	
I wouldn't have waited **Eu não teria esperado**	I didn't wait **Eu não esperei**			

Negation

Example: <u>To Run / Correr</u> (Infinitive Verb)

Present	Gerund	Future	Past Participle	Conditional
I don't run	I am not running	I won't run	I haven't run	I wouldn't run
Eu não corro	**Eu não estou correndo**	**Eu não irei correr**	**Eu não já correi**	**Eu não corraria**

I won't be running		I wasn't running		I don't have run		I haven't been running
Eu não estarei correndo		**Eu não estava correndo**		**Eu não tenho que correr**		**Eu não tenho estado correndo**

I wouldn't have run	I didn't run
Eu não teria corrido	**Eu não corri**

Example: <u>To Eat / Comer</u> (Infinitive Verb)

Present	Gerund	Future	Past Participle	Conditional
I don't eat	I am not eating	I won't eat	I haven't eaten	I wouldn't eat
Eu não como	**Eu não estou comendo**	**Eu não irei comer**	**Eu não já comi**	**Eu não comeria**

I won't be eating	I wasn't eating	I don't have to eat	I haven't been eating
Eu não estarei comendo	**Eu não estava comando**	**Eu não tenho que comer**	**Eu não tenho estado comendo**

I wouldn't have eaten	I didn't eat
Eu não teria comido	**Eu não comi**

Negation

Example: <u>To Talk / Falar</u> (Infinitive Verb)

Present I don't talk **Eu não falo**	Gerund I am not talking **Eu não estou falando**	Future I won't talk **Eu não irei falar**	Past Participle I haven't talked **Eu não já falei**	Conditional I wouldn't talk **Eu não falaria**
I won't be talking **Eu não estarei falando**	I wasn't talking **Eu não estava falando**	I don't have to talk **Eu não tenho que falar**	I haven't been talking **Eu não tenho estado falando**	
I wouldn't have spoken **Eu não teria falado**	I didn't speak **Eu não falei**			

Example: <u>To Call / Chamar</u> (Infinitive Verb)

Present I don't call **Eu não chamo**	Gerund I am not calling **Eu não estou chamando**	Future I won't call **Eu não irei chamar**	Past Participle I haven't called **Eu não já chamei**	Conditional I wouldn't call **Eu não chamaria**
I won't be calling **Eu não estarei chamando**	I wasn't calling **Eu não estava chamando**	I don't have to call **Eu não tenho que chamar**	I haven't been calling **Eu não tenho estado chamando**	
I wouldn't have called **Eu não teria chamado**	I didn't call **Eu não chamei**			

Negation

Example: To Take / Levar (Infinitive Verb)

Present I don't take **Eu não levo**	Gerund I am not taking **Eu não estou levando**	Future I won't take **Eu não irei levar**	Past Participle I haven't taken **Eu não já levei**	Conditional I wouldn't take **Eu não levaria**
I won't be taking **Eu não estarei levando**	I wasn't taking **Eu não estava levando**	I don't have to take **Eu não tenho que levar**		I haven't been taking **Eu não tenho estado levando**
I wouldn't have taken **Eu não teria levado**	I didn't take **Eu não levei**			

Example: To Get / Receber (Infinitive Verb)

Present I don't get **Eu não recebo**	Gerund I am not getting **Eu não estou recebendo**	Future I won't get **Eu não irei receber**	Past Participle I haven't gotten **Eu não já recebi**	Conditional I wouldn't get **Eu não receberia**
I won't be getting **Eu não estarei recebendo**	I wasn't getting **Eu não estava recebendo**	I don't have to get **Eu não tenho que receber**		I haven't been getting **Eu não tenho estado recebendo**
I wouldn't have gotten **Eu não teria recebido**	I didn't get **Eu não recebi**			

Negation

Example: <u>To Think / Pensar</u> (Infinitive Verb)

Present	Gerund	Future	Past Participle	Conditional
I don't think	I am not thinking	I won't think	I haven't thought	I wouldn't think
Eu não penso	**Eu não estou pensando**	**Eu não irei pensar**	**Eu não já pensei**	**Eu não pensaria**
I won't be thinking	I wasn't thinking	I didn't have to think	I haven't been thinking	
Eu não estarei pensando	**Eu não estaba pensando**	**Eu não tenho que pensar**	**Eu não tenho estado pensando**	
I wouldn't have thought	I didn't think			
Eu não teria pensado	**Eu não pensei**			

Example: <u>To Study / Estudar</u> (Infinitive Verb)

Present	Gerund	Future	Past Participle	Conditional
I don't study	I am not studying	I won't study	I haven't studied	I wouldn't study
Eu não estudo	**Eu não estou estudando**	**Eu não irei estudar**	**Eu não já estudei**	**Eu não estudaria**
I won't be studying	I wasn't studying	I didn't have to study	I haven't been studyting	
Eu não estarei estudando	**Eu não estava estudando**	**Eu não tenho que estudar**	**Eu não tenho estado estudando**	
I wouldn't have studied	I didn't study			
Eu não teria estudado	**Eu não estudei**			

Negation

Example: <u>To Write / Escrever</u> (Infinitive Verb)

Present I don't write **Eu não escrevo**	Gerund I am not writing **Eu não estou escrevendo**	Future I won't write **Eu não irei escrevar**	Past Participle I haven't written **Eu não já escrevi**	Conditional I wouldn't write **Eu não escreveria**
I won't be writing **Eu não estarei escrevendo**	I wasn't writing **Eu não estaba escrevendo**	I didn't have to write **Eu não tenho que escrever**	I haven't been writing **Eu não tenho estado escrevendo**	
I wouldn't have wrote **Eu não teria escrito**	I didn't write **Eu não escrevei**			

Example: <u>To Read / Ler</u> (Infinitive Verb)

Present I don't read **Eu não leio**	Gerund I am not reading **Eu não estou lendo**	Future I won't read **Eu não irei ler**	Past Participle I haven't read **Eu não tenho lido**	Conditional I wouldn't read **Eu não leria**
I won't be reading **Eu não estarei lendo**	I wasn't reading **Eu não estava lendo**	I didn't have to read **Eu não tenho que ler**	I haven't been reading **Eu não tenho estado lendo**	
I wouldn't have read **Eu não teria lido**	I didn't read **Eu não leio**			

Negation

Example: <u>To Do / Fazer</u> (Infinitive Verb)

Present	Gerund	Future	Past Participle	Conditional
I don't do	I am not doing	I won't do	I haven't done	I wouldn't do
Eu não faço	**Eu não estou fazendo**	**Eu não irei fazar**	**Eu não já fiz**	**Eu não faria**
I won't be doing	I wasn't doing	I didn't have to do	I haven't been doing	
Eu não estarei fazendo	**Eu não estaba fazendo**	**Eu não tenho que fazer**	**Eu não tenho estado fazendo**	
I wouldn't have done	I didn't do			
Eu não teria feito	**Eu não fiz**			

Example: <u>To Work / Trabalhar</u> (Infinitive Verb)

Present	Gerund	Future	Past Participle	Conditional
I don't work	I am not working	I won't work	I haven't worked	I wouldn't work
Eu não trabalho	**Eu não estou trabalhando**	**Eu não irei trabalhar**	**Eu não já trabalhado**	**Eu não trabalharia**
I won't be working	I wasn't working	I didn't have to work	I haven't been working	
Eu não estarei trabalhando	**Eu não estava trabalhando**	**Eu não tenho que trabalhar**	**Eu não tenho estado trabalhando**	
I wouldn't have worked	I didn't work			
Eu não teria trabalhado	**Eu não trabalhei**			

Questions

Example: <u>To Cook / Cozinhar</u> (Infinitive Verb)

Present	Gerund	Future	Past Participle	Conditional
Do I cook? **Eu cozinho?**	Am I cooking? **Eu estou cozinhando?**	Will I cook? **Eu irei cozinhar?**	Have I cooked? **Eu já cozinhei?**	Would I cook? **Eu cozinharia?**
Will I be cooking? **Eu estarei cozinhando?**	Was I cooking? **Eu estava cozinhando?**	Do I have to cook? **Eu tenho que cozinhar?**	Have I been cooking? **Eu tenho estado cozinhando?**	
Would I have cooked? **Eu teria cozinhado?**	Did I cook? **Eu cozinhei?**			

Example: <u>To Wait / Esperar</u> (Infinitive Verb)

Present	Gerund	Future	Past Participle	Conditional
Do I wait? **Eu espero?**	Am I waiting? **Eu estou esperando?**	Will I wait? **Eu irei esperar?**	Have I waited? **Eu tenho esperado?**	Would I wait? **Eu esperaria?**
Will I be waiting? **Eu vou estar esperando?**	Was I waiting? **Eu estava esperando?**	Do I have to wait? **Eu tenho que esperar?**	Have I been waiting? **Eu tenho estado esperando?**	
Would I have waited? **Eu teria esperado?**	Did I wait? **Eu esperei?**			

Questions

Example: <u>To Run / Correr</u> (Infinitive Verb)

Present	Gerund	Future	Past Participle	Conditional
Do I run? **Eu corro?**	Am I running? **Eu estou correndo?**	Will I run? **Eu irei correr?**	Have I run **Eu já correi?**	Would I run? **Eu corraria?**
Will I be running? **Eu estarei correndo?**	Was I running? **Eu estava correndo?**	Do I have to run? **Eu tenho que correr?**	Have I been running? **Eu tenho estado correndo?**	
Would I have run? **Eu teria corrido?**	Did I run? **Eu corri?**			

Example: <u>To Eat / Comer</u> (Infinitive Verb)

Present	Gerund	Future	Past Participle	Conditional
Do I eat? **Eu como?**	Am I eating? **Eu estou comendo?**	Will I eat? **Eu irei comer?**	Have I eaten? **Eu já comi?**	Would I eat? **Eu comeria?**
Will be eating? **Eu estarei comendo?**	Was I eating? **Eu estava comando?**	Do I have to eat? **Eu tenho que comer?**	Have I been eating? **Eu tenho estado comendo?**	
Would I have eaten? **Eu teria comido?**	Did I eat? **Eu comi?**			

Questions

Example: <u>To Talk / Falar</u> (Infinitive Verb)

The Four Templates

Present Do I talk? **Eu falo?**	**Gerund** Am I talking? **Eu estou falando?**	**Future** Will I talk? **Eu irei falar?**	**Past Participle** Have I talked? **Eu já falei?**	**Conditional** Would I talk? **Eu filaria?**
Will I be talking? **Eu estarei falando?**	Was I talking? **Eu estava falando?**	Did I have to talk? **Eu tenho que falar?**		Have I been talking? **Eu tenho estado falando?**
Would I have spoken? **Eu teria falado?**	Did I talk? **Eu falei?**			

Example: <u>To Call / Chamar</u> (Infinitive Verb)

The Four Templates

Present Do I call? **Eu chamo?**	**Gerund** Am I calling? **Eu estou chamando?**	**Future** Will I call? **Eu irei chamar?**	**Past Participle** Have I called? **Eu já chamei?**	**Conditional** Would I call? **Eu chamaria?**
Will I be calling? **Eu estarei chamando?**	Was I calling? **Eu estava chamando?**	Did I have to call? **Eu tenho que chamar?**		Have I been calling? **Eu tenho estado chamando?**
Would I have called? **Eu teria chamado?**	Did I call? **Eu chamei?**			

Questions

Example: <u>To Take / Levar</u> (Infinitive Verb)

Present	Gerund	Future	Past Participle	Conditional
Do I take?	Am I taking?	Will I take?	Have I taken?	Would I take?
Eu levo?	**Eu estou levando?**	**Eu irei levar?**	**Eu já levei?**	**Eu levaria?**

Will I be taking?	Was I taking?	Do I have to take?	Have I been taking?
Eu estarei levando?	**Eu estava levando?**	**Eu tenho que levar?**	**Eu tenho estado levando?**
Would I have taken?	Did I take?		
Eu teria levado?	**Eu levei?**		

Example: <u>To Get / Receber</u> (Infinitive Verb)

Present	Gerund	Future	Past Participle	Conditional
Do I get?	Am I getting?	Will I get?	Have I gotten?	Would I get?
Eu recebo?	**Eu estou recebendo?**	**Eu irei receber?**	**Eu já recebi?**	**Eu receberia?**

Will I be getting?	Was I getting?	Do I have to get?	Have I been getting?
Eu estarei recebendo?	**Eu estava recebendo?**	**Eu tenho que receber?**	**Eu tenho estado recebendo?**
Would I have gotten?	Did I get?		
Eu teria recebido?	**Eu recebi?**		

Questions

Example: <u>To Think / Pensar</u> (Infinitive Verb)

The Four Templates

Present Do I think? **Eu penso?**	**Gerund** Am I thinking? **Eu estou pensando?**	**Future** Will I think? **Eu irei pensar?**	**Past Participle** Have I thought? **Eu já pensei?**	**Conditional** Would I think? **Eu pensaria?**
Will I be thinking? **Eu estarei pensando?**	Was I thinking? **Eu estaba pensando?**	Do I have to think? **Eu tenho que pensar?**		Have I been thinking? **Eu tenho estado pensando?**
Would I have thought? **Eu teria pensado?**	Did I think? **Eu pensei?**			

Example: <u>To Study / Estudar</u> (Infinitive Verb)

The Four Templates

Present Do I study? **Eu estudo?**	**Gerund** Am I studying? **Eu estou estudando?**	**Future** Will I study? **Eu irei estudar?**	**Past Participle** Have I studied? **Eu já estudei?**	**Conditional** Would I study? **Eu estudaria?**
Will I be studying? **Eu estarei estudando?**	Was I studying? **Eu estava estudando?**	Do I have to study? **Eu tenho que estudar?**		Have I been studyting? **Eu tenho estado estudando?**
Would I have studied? **Eu teria estudado?**	Did I study? **Eu estudei?**			

Questions

Example: To Write / Escrever (Infinitive Verb)   The Four Templates

Present	Gerund	Future	Past Participle	Conditional
Do I write? **Eu escrevo?**	Am I writing? **Eu estou escrevendo?**	Will I write? **Eu irei escrevar?**	Have I written? **Eu já escrevi?**	Would I write? **Eu escreveria?**
Will I be writing? **Eu estarei escrevendo?**	Was I writing? **Eu estaba escrevendo?**	Do I have to write? **Eu tenho que escrever?**	Have I been writing? **Eu tenho estado escrevendo?**	
Would I have written? **Eu teria escrito?**	Did I write? **Eu escrevei?**			

Example: To Read / Ler (Infinitive Verb)   The Four Templates

Present	Gerund	Future	Past Participle	Conditional
Do I read? **Eu leio?**	Am I reading? **Eu estou lendo?**	Will I read? **Eu irei ler?**	Have I read? **Eu tenho lido?**	Would I read? **Eu leria?**
Will I be reading? **Eu estarei lendo?**	Was I reading? **Eu estava lendo?**	Do I have to read? **Eu tenho que ler?**	Have I been reading? **Eu tenho estado lendo?**	
Would I have read? **Eu teria lido?**	Did I read? **Eu leio?**			

Questions

Example: <u>To Do / Fazer</u> (Infinitive Verb)

Present	Gerund	Future	Past Participle	Conditional
Do I do?	Am I doing?	Will I do?	Have I done?	Would I do?
Eu faço?	**Eu estou fazendo?**	**Eu irei fazar?**	**Eu já fiz?**	**Eu faria?**
Will I be doing?		Was I doing?	Do I have to do?	Have I been doing?
Eu estarei fazendo?		**Eu estaba fazendo?**	**Eu tenho que fazer?**	**Eu tenho estado fazendo?**
Would I have done?		Did I do?		
Eu teria feito?		**Eu fiz?**		

Example: <u>To Work / Trabalhar</u> (Infinitive Verb)

Present	Gerund	Future	Past Participle	Conditional
Do I work?	Am I working?	Will I work?	Have I worked?	Would I work?
Eu trabalho?	**Eu estou trabalhando?**	**Eu irei trabalhar?**	**Eu já trabalhado?**	**Eu trabalharia?**
Will I be working?		Was I working?	Do I have to work?	Have I been working?
Eu estarei trabalhando?		**Eu estava trabalhando?**	**Eu tenho que trabalhar?**	**Eu tenho estado trabalhando?**
Would I have worked?		Did I work?		
Eu teria trabalhado?		**Eu trabalhei?**		

Portuguese Vocabulary

Vocabulary

A

A little: um pouco
A: um
A lot: muito
About: sobre
Above: acima
Ache: dor
Address: adereço
Airport: aeroporto
After: depois
Afternoon: tarde
Afterwards: mais tarde
Again: outra vez
Ago: atrás
Aid: ajuda
Air: ar
Airline: linha aérea
Airplane: avião
All: tudo
Almost: quase
Alone: sozinho
Already: já
Also: também
Always: sempre
Amusing: divertido
And: e
Annoy: incomodar, irritar
Another: outro

Anybody: qualquer um
Anyone: alguém
Apple: maçã
April: abril
Arrest: prender
Arrival: chegada
At (Place): no lugar
At (Hour): em hora
Automobile: automóvel
Autumn: outono
Awful: horrível
August: agost

B

Baggage: bagagem
Bad: mau
Baked: cozido
Bakery: padaria
Bank: banco
Barely: por pouco
Bargains: pechinchas
Bathroom: banheiro
Because: porque
Bed: cama
Bed Cover: cobertor
Beef: carne, bife
Beer: cerveja
Behind: atras
Between: entre
Bicycle: bicicleta

Black: negro, preto
Blood: sangre
Blue: azul
Boat: barco
Book: livro
Boss: chefe
Bottle: garrafa
Box: caixa
Boy: rapaz, garoto, menino
Bread: pão
Breakdown: separação
Breakfast: pequeno almoço
British: britânico
Brown: castanho
Bulb: lâmpada
Bull: touro
Bus: ônibus
Busy: ocupado
But: mas
Butter: manteiga
Button: botão
By the way: a propósito

C

Calf: bezerro
Canteen: cantina
Car: carro
Careful: cuidado
Cart: carrinho
Caution: cuidado

Vocabulary

Cents: centavos
Cereal: cereal
Change: troco
Cheap: barato
Cheese: queijo
Cherry: cereja
Chest: peito
Chicken: frango
Child: criança
Chocolate: chocolate
Church: igreja
Cigarette Lighter: isqueiro
Clean: limpo
Clock: relojo
Clothes: roupas
Class: classe
Close: perto
Coat: casaco
Coal: carvão
Coffee: café
Cold: frio
Complete: completo
Concert: concerto
Corner: canto
Cream: creme
Cup: copo
Curve: curva
Customs: aduana

D

Daily: diário
Ladies: senhoras
Dance: dançar
Danger: perigo
Dark: escuro
Day: dia
Dead: morto
Dear: querido
December: dezembro
Dentist: dentista
Department Store: loja
Departure: partida
Dinner: jantar
Discount: desconto
Desert: deserto
Despite: embora
Dessert: sobremessa
Detour: desvio
Diapers: fraldas
Dictionary: dicionário
Dining room: sala de jantar
Dirty: sujo
Dizzy: tonto,tonta
Down: baixo
Dozen: dúzia
Dress: vestido
Drip (Leak): filtragem
Drugstore: farmacia

E

Each: cada
Early: cedo
Egg: ovo
Either: qualquer
Electricity: electricidade
Eleven: onze
Embassy: embaixada
Emergency: emergência
Empty: vazio
England: Inglaterra
Entrance: entrada
Error: erro
Evening: noite
Even though: mesmo assim
Every: todo
Everybody: todos
Exchange: intercâmbio
Excursion: excursão
Excuse (me): desculpa
Exit: saida
Expensive: caro
Eye: olho
Eye Glasses:

F

Fair: Juro
Family: familia
Far: longe

Vocabulary

Fast: rápido
Father: pai
Faucet: torneira
Fault: culpa
February: fevereiro
Fever: febre
Film: filme
Fine: bom
Fire: fogo
First: primeiro
Fish: peixe
Flag: bandeira
Flight: vôo
Fly: voar
Food: comer
Foot: pé
For: para
Forbidden: proibido
Fork: garfo
Forty: quarenta
Four: quatro
Fourteen: catorze
Fourth: quarto
Free: gratis
Fresh water: agua fresca
Friday: sexta feira
Fried: frito
Friend: amigo, amiga
Friendly: amigável

From: de
Fruit: fruta
Funny: engraçado

G

Game: jogo
Garlic: alho
Gas: gas
Gasoline: gasolina
Generally: geralmente
Gentleman: cavalheiro
Gift: presente
Girl: rapariga, menina
Glove: luva
Good: bom
Gray: cinza
Green: verde
Greetings: cumprimentos
Guide: guia

H

Half: metade
Ham: fiambre
Handbag: bolsa
Happy: feliz
Headache: dor de cabeça
Heart: coração
Heat: calor
Heavy: pesado
Hello: olá

Help: ajuda
Here: aqui
Hospital: hospital
Hot: quente
Hour: hora
How: como
How far: quão longe
How long: quanto tempo
How much: quanto
Hot: quente
Hundred: cem
Husband: marido

I

Ice cream: gelado
If: se
Immediately: imediatamente
In: em
Included: incluido
Infant: criança
Information: informação
Inside: dentro
Introduce: introduzir

J

Jam: geléia
January: janeiro
Jewelry: jóias
Juice: juicio
July: julio

Vocabulary

K

Keep: guardar
Key: chave
Kind: agradável
Kitchen: cozinha
Knife: faca

L

Lady: lady
Large: grande
Last: ultimo
Late: tarde
Lavatory: lavabo
Laxative: laxantes
Least: ultimo
Leather: couro
Left: sobras
Legal: legal
Lemon: limão
Lemonade: limonada
Less: menos
Letter: carta
Lettuce: lechuga
List: lista
Little: pouco
Low: baixo
Lunch:

N

Nothing: nada
Notice: perceber
November: novembro
Now: agora
Number: numero

M

Machine: maquina
Madam: dona
Made in: fabricado em
Magazine: revista
Mail: correio
Manager: manager
Many: muitos
Map: mapa
March: marzo
Matches: fósforos
May: mayo
May be: poderia ser
Meal: refeição
Men: homen
Merely: apenas
Meat: carne
Menu: menu
Message: menssagem
Middle: meio
Midnight: meia noite
Milk: leite

Minute: minuto
Miss: sra.
Mister: sr.
Monday: segunda feira
Money: dinheiro
Money Order: ordem de pagamento
Month: mês
Morning: manhã
Mother: mãe
Motorcycle: motocicleta
Movie: filme
Mr.: sr
Mrs.: sra
Much: muito
Museum: museu

N

Napkin: guardanapo
Nationality: nacionalidade
Naturally: naturalmente
Near: perto
Neither: nenhum
Never: nunca
Next: próxima
Next to: perto de
Night: noite
Nightclub: discoteca, boate
Nine: nove
Nineteen: dezenove
Ninety: noventa

Vocabulary

Ninth: nona
No: não
Noise: barulho
None: nenhum
Noon: meio dia
Not: não

O

October: outubro
Of course: claro
Office: escritório
Often: frequentemente
Okay: ok
Omelet: tortilha
On: sobre
Once: uma vez
One: uma
One Hundred: cem
Only: só
On sale: à venta
Open: aberto
Orange: laranja
Otherwise: por outro lado
Outside: fora
Over: acima
Overcoat: sobretudo

P

Doorman: porteiro
Maybe : puede ser

Padaria: Bakery
Diapers: fraldas
Father: pai
For: para
Stop: pare
Park: parque
Ticket: passagem, bilhete
Potatoes: batatas
Toilet paper: papel higiénico
Umbrella: guarda-chuva
Passport: passaporte
Payment: pagamento
Movie: filme
Small, Little: pequeno
Per day: por dia
Of course: claro
Dessert: sobremesa
Excuse me: com licença
But: mas
Heavy: pesado
Passenger: passageiro

Q

Dear: querido
Cheese: queijo
Maybe: talvez
What, that: o que

R

Radiator: Radiador

Railroad: ferrovia
Rain: chuva
Raincoat: capa de chuva
Razor Blade: navalha
Ready: preparado
Receipt: recibo
Record: registro
Red: vermelho
Repeat: repetir
Reserved: reservado
Rest Room: banheiro
Rice: arroz
Right: direito, certo
Right away: agora mesmo
Right now: agora mesmo
Roast Beef: carne assada
Roasted: assado
Round Trip: ida e volta

S

Salad: salada
Sale: venda
Salty: salgado
Saturday: sábado
School: escola
Seat: cadeira
Second: segundo
See you later: até logo
September: setembro

Vocabulary

Service: serviço
Seven: sete
Seventh: séptimo
Seventeen: dezesete
Seventy: setenta
Several: varios
Shebert: sorvete
Ship: barco
Shopping: compras
Show Me: mostra-me
Shower: chuveiro
Shrimp: camarão
Sick: doente
Sir: senhor
Six: seis
Sixteen: dezeseis
Sixth: sexto
Sixty: sessenta
Slow: devagar
Small: pequeno
Smoker: fumador
Snack: lanche
Soap: sabão
Soon: pronto
Soup: sopa
Somebody: alguém
Someone: alguém
Spoon: culher

Sports: esporte
Spring: primavera
Spring (season): primavera
Station: estação
Stewardess: aeromoça
Sticker: adesivo
Still: ainda
Stop: para
Store: loja
Strawberry: morango
Street: rua
Subway: metrô
Sugar: açúcar
Suitcase: mala
Summer: verão
Sunday: domingo
Sure: claro

T

Table: mesa
Tablet: tablete
Tailor: alfaiate
Tap: toque
Tea: chá
Teaspoon: culher de chá
Telegram: telegrama
Telephone: telefone
Television: televisão
Ten: dez

Thank you: obrigado
Theft: robo
There: ali
There is/are: tem, está
Thermometer: termómetro
Thief: ladrão
Thing: coisa
Third: terceiro
Thirteen: treze
Thirty: trinta
This evening: esta noite
Thousand: mil
Three: três
Through: por meio de
Thursday: quinta feira
Tuesday: terça feira
Ticket: bilhete
Time (Hour): tempo (hora)
Timetable: calendário
Tip (gratuity): gorjeta, dica
To: para
Toast (bread): tostada
Tabacco: tabaco
Today: hoje
Toilet paper: papel higiênico
Toilet: banheiro
Tomorrow: amanhã
Tonight: esta noite
Too (Also): também

Vocabulary

Tourism: turismo
Tourist: turista
Towel: toalha
Track: seguir
Traffic: tráfico
Train: comboio
Tuesday: terça feira
TV Set: Televisão
Twelve: doze
Twenty: vinte
Twice: duas vezes
Two: dois
Two hundred: duzentos
Typewriter: máquina de escrever

U

Umbrella: guarda-chuva
Under: embaixo
Underneath: debaixo
Understood: entendido, percebido
United States: Estados Unidos
Until: até
Up: acima
Urgent: urgente
Unless: a não ser
Unwilling: relutante

V

Vacant: vacante
Valuable: valioso

Vanilla: baunilha
Veal: vitela
Vegetables: vegetais
Very: muito
Vinegar: vinagre

W

Waiter: garçon
Waitress: garçonete
Waiting Room: sala de espera
Wallet: carteira
Warm: morno
Watch out: atenção
Water: agua
Watermelon: melancia
Wednesday: quarta feira
Week: semana
Weekly: semanalmente
Welcome: Bem-vindo
Well: bem
Wet paint: nós pintamos
What: o que
When: quando
Whenever: qualquer hora
Where: onde
Where to: para onde
Wherever: qualquer lugar
Which: qual

Whichever: qualquer
White: branco
Who: quem
Whoever: quem quer
Whom: quem
Whose: de quem
Why: porque
Wide: largo
Wife: esposa, mulher
Willing: disposto
Window: janela
Wine: vinho
Winter: iverno
With: com
Woman: mulher
Women: mulheres
Word: palavra
Wristwatch: relógio de pulso

Y

Year: ano
Yellow: amarelo
Yes: sim
Yesterday: ontem
Yet: ainda
Yield: recolher

Z

Zipper: zíper

Notes

Gerund / (Gerundio): Verb in Gerund required the verb "To Be" to precede them, in Portuguese that would the verb "ser". To practice building phrases in Gerund (Action), simply place the Verb To Be "Ser" just before the Gerund Verb using the following conjugations.

(I am) – Eu sou/estoy

(You are) – Tu és

(He is) – Ele é/está

(She is) – Ela é/está

(We are) – Nós somos/estamos

(You are) – Vocês são/estão

(They are) – Eles são/estão

(It is) – Isso é/está

Examples:

I Am Writing – **Eu Estou Escrevendo**

You Are Waiting – **Tu estás esperando**

He is Calling – **Ele está chamando**

She Is Cooking – **Ela está cozinhando**

We Are Eating – **Nós estamos comendo**

You Are Eating – **Eles estão comendo**

They Are Coming – **Eles estão chegando**

Notes

Participle (Participio): Verbs in Participle require the verb "To Have" to precede them, in Portuguese that would be the verb **"Ter"**. To practice building phrases in Gerund (Past), simply place the Verb To Have **"Ter"** just before the Participle

Verb using the following conjugations:

(I am) – Eu tenho

(You are) – Tú tens

(He is) – Ele tem

(She is) – Ela tem

(We are) – Nós temos

(You are) – Vós tendes

(They are) – têm

(It is) – tem

Examples:

I have Waited – **Eu Tenho Esperado**

You Have Gotten Mail – **Tu Tens Recebido Correio**

She Has Slept Well – **Ela Tem Dormido Bem**

He Has Eaten Late – **Ele Tem Comido Tarde**

We have run in the morning – **Nós temos corrido pela manhã**

You have gone to class early – **Vocês têm ido às aulas mais cedo**

They Have done the Homework together – **Eles têm feito os deveres de casa juntos**

Notes

In Portuguese sometimes you use the letter "A" between infinitive verbs.

Examples:

I can go to eat later – **Eu posso ir a comer mais tarde**

I want to come to visit you next week – **Eu quero ir a visitar-te na próxima semana**

I have to go to eat – **Eu tenho que ir a comer**

On the Next Page
You'll Find A
List Of,

Verbos Infinitivos
Infinitive Verbs

Study, Read and Spell them multiple times
'till they stick and……
Notice that all of them (well almost all)

Start with To_____in English
End with _____R in Spanish

Lesson 4: Part 4

A
To Accept: Aceptar
To Acquire: Adquirir
To Allow: Permitir
To Announce: Anunciar
To Answer: Responder
To Argue: Discutir
To Approve: Aprobar
To Arrive: Llegar
To Arrange: Arreglar
To Ask: Preguntar, Pedir
To Assist: Asistir

B
To Be: Estar
To Be: Ser
To Be Angry: Estar Molesto
To Be Right: Acertar
To Be Thankful: Agradecer
To Be Wrong: Equivocar
To Become: Convertir
To Begin: Empezar
To Believe: Creer
To Bring: Traer
To Build: Construir
To Buy: Comprar

C
To Cause: Causar
To Call: Llamar
Can: Poder
To Clean: Limpiar
To Close: Cerrar
To Collect: Cobrar
To Come: Venir
To Complete: Completar
To Cook: Cocinar
To Copy: Copiar
To Correct: Corregir
Could: Podria
To Cry: Llorar

D
To Dance: Bailar
To Depart: Partir
To Discuss: Discutir
To Do: Hacer
To Doubt: Dudar
To Dress: Vestir
To Drink: Beber
To Drive: Manejar

E
To Earn: Ganar

To Eat: Comer
To Enter: Entrar
To Erase: Borrar
To Exit: Salir

F
To Fall: Caer
To Fear: Temer
To Feel: Sentir
To Find: Encontrar
To Find Out: Averiguar
To Finish: Terminar
To Fit: Caber
To Follow: Seguir
To Forget: Olvidar
To Forgive: Perdonar

G
To Get: Adquirir
To Get: Conseguir
To Get: Lograr
To Get: Obtener
To Get: Recibir
To Give: Dar
To Go: ir
To Greet: Recibir
To Grow: Crecer

L
To Laugh: Reir
To Learn: Aprender
To Leave: Partir
To Lend: Prestar
To Listen: Oir
To Let; Dejar
To Like: Gustar
To Live: Vivir
To Look: Mirar
To Look (like): Parecer
To Lose: Perder
To Love: Amar
To Live: Vivir
To Look: Mirar
To Look (like): Parecer
To Lose: Perder
To Love: Amar

M
May: Poder
To Make: Hacer
To Move: Mover
Must: Deber

Lesson 4: Part 4

N
To Name: Nombrar
To Need: Necesitar
To Nix: Negar, Prohibir
(Slang)

O
To Obey: Obedecer
To Offer: Ofrecer
To Observe: Observar
To Open: Abrir
To Order: Ordenar
To Owe: Deber
To Own: Poseer

P
To Pardon: Perdonar
To Pay: Pagar
To Pick(select): Escoger
To Pick: Recoger
To Play (instrument): Tocar
To Pull: Halar
To Purchase: Comprar
To Push: Empujar
To Put: Poner

R
To Read: Leer
To Realize: Darse cuenta
To Refuse: Reusar
To Reject: Rechazar
To Remember: Recordar
To Repeat: Repetir
To Reply: Responder
To Request: Solicitar
To Respect: Respetar
To Rest: Descansar
To Return: Regresar
To Run Correr

S
To Save: Salvar
To Satisfy: Satisfacer
To Say: Decir
To See: Ver
To Seek: Buscar:
To Sell: Vender
To Send: Enviar
Shall: Deber
Should: Debería
To Show: Mostrar, Presentar
To Shop: Ir de compras
To Sit: Sentar

To Sleep: Dormir
To Smile: Sonreir
To Solve: Solucionar
To Speak: Hablar
To Start: Empezar
To Study: Estudiar

T
To Take: Tomar
To Take: Llevar
To Talk: Hablar
To Teach: Enseñar
To Tell: Decir
To Terminate: Terminar
To Thank: Agradecer
To Think: Pensar
To Travel: Viajar
To Trot: Trotar
To Try: Tratar

U
To Understand : Entender
To Use: Usar
To Utilize: Utilizar

V
To Value; Valorar
To Visit: Visitar

W
To Wait: Esperar
To Walk: Caminar
To Want: Querer
To Wash: Lavar
To Watch: Mirar
To Wear: Usar
To Wish: Desear
To Win: Ganar
To Work: Trabajar
To Write: Escribir

Y
To Yawn: Bostezar

Z
To Zip: Cerrar

Learning Step 7

The '4' Trigger verbs

enable you to initiate any basic conversation

Practice them, especially the conjugations and the pronunciation

The following 4 "Trigger Verbs"
Enable you to initiate most conversations

Lesson No. 5	**Lesson No. 6**
To be	To have
Ser/Estar	Tener/ Haber
Lesson No. 7	**Lesson No. 8**
To want	Can
Querer	Poder

Lesson 5: Part 1

The 1st. Trigger Verb is "To Be"
It has two meanings in Spanish: "Ser" (Sehr) or "Estar" (Ehstahr)

Let us first review the Verb "Ser" (Sehr) :
"Ser" describes a quasi-permanent situation ,
meaning a permanent or an almost permanent situation or condition.

Examples of "SER" (SEHR)

SER (SEHR)			I	am	tall	He	is	a policeman
(I)	Yo	Soy (Sohee)	Yo	soy	alto	El	es	un policía
(You)	Usted	Es (Ehs)	**She**	**is**	**smart**	**You**	**are**	**single**
(He)	El	Es (Ehs)	Ella	es	lista	Usted	es	soltero
(She)	Ella	Es (Ehs)	**They**	**are**	**fanatics**	**He**	**is**	**late**
(We)	Nosotros	Somos	Ellos	son	fanáticos	El	está	tarde
(They)	Ellos	Son (Sohn)	**It**	**is**	**late**	**She**	**is**	**beautiful**
(it)	Eso, Esto	Es (Ehs).	Es	tarde		Ella	es	bella

Lesson 5: Part 2

The 1st. Trigger Verb is "To Be"
It has two meanings in Spanish: "Ser" (Sehr) or "Estar" (Ehstahr)

Let us now review the Verb " Estar" (Est hahr)
"Estar" describes a transitory situation or condition (something passing).

Examples of "ESTAR" (EHSTAHR)

ESTAR/(EHSTAHR)		**I**	**am**	**angry**	**They**	**are**	**ready**
(I) Yo	Estoy (Estoee)	Yo	estoy	molesto	Ellos	están	listos
(You) Usted	Esta (Ehstah)	**You**	**are**	**late**	**She**	**is**	**sick**
(He) El	Esta (Ehstah)	Usted	está	tarde	Ella	está	enferma
(She) Ella	Esta (Ehstah)	**He**	**is**	**tired**	**You**	**are**	**out**
(We) Nosotros	Estamos	El	está	cansado	Usted	está	afuera
(They) Ellos	Estan (Ehstan)	**She**	**is**	**wrong**	**It**	**is**	**right**
(It) Eso/Esto	Esta	Ella	esta	equivocada	Es	lo	correcto

Lesson 5: Part 3

The Trigger Verbs: To be =Ser o Estar

Examples of verb **"Ser"** (Quasi-permanent situation)	Examples of verb **"Estar"** (temporary situation)
I am a good player Yo soy un buen jugador	**I am eating early each day** Yo estoy comiendo temprano cada día
I am a great person Yo soy una gran persona	**I am waiting for you now** Yo estoy esperando por usted ahora
You are a good man Usted es un buen hombre	**You are tired every day** Usted está cansado todos los días
You are a disgusting person Usted es una persona desagradable	**You are upset about the game** Usted está molesto acerca del juego
He is an excellent student El es un estudiante excelente	**He is taking them to the airport** El los está llevando al aeropuerto
He is a fantastic cook El es un cocinero fantástico	**He is going to visit you this weekend** El está yendo a visitarle este fin de semana
We are always here for you Nosotros estamos siempre aquí para usted	**She is coming home for Thanksgiving** Ella está viniendo a casa en Acción de Gracias
We are the same people Nosotros somos la misma gente	**We are thinking about you** Nosotros estamos pensando acerca de usted
You are a winning team Ustedes son un equipo ganador	**You are frustrated by the whole situation** Usted está frustrado por toda la situación
You are never on time Ustedes nunca están a tiempo	**They are very tired after the trip** Ellos están muy cansados después del viaje
They are the best in town Ellos son los mejores en la ciudad	**It is getting late** Se está haciendo tarde
They are the worst there is Ellos son lo peor que hay	**We are doing our homework** Nosotros estamos haciendo nuestra tarea
It is better if you don't come Es mejor si usted no viene	**She is trying to finish her task today** Ella está tratando de finalizar su tarea hoy

The 2nd Trigger Verb is "To Have"
It has two meanings in Spanish: "Tener" (tehnehr) o "Haber" (ahbehr)

Let us review first the Verb "Tener" (Tehnehr) in Spanish.
"Tener" has two meanings in Spanish:
    1) Tener (tehnehr) which describes either ownership/hold/possession or
    2) Tener (tehner) que (keh) which denotes duty/responsibility

<u>Examples using Tener (tehnehr) and Tener (tehnehr) que (keh)</u>

<u>Tener</u> (tehnehr)	<u>Describiendo propiedad</u>		<u>Describiendo responsabilidad</u>		
(I) Yo tengo (tehngoh)	**I**	**have an automobile**	**I**	**have**	**to go to eat**
(You) Usted tiene (tee-ehne)	Yo	tengo un coche	Yo	tengo "que"	ir a comer
(He) tiene (tee-ehne)	**He**	**has an extended family**	**I**	**have to**	**talk with him**
(She) Ella tiene (tee-ehne)	El	tiene una familia numerosa	Yo	tengo "que"	hablar con él
(We) Nosotros tenemos	**You**	**have a problem**	**He**	**has to**	**take you home**
(You) Ustedes tienen	Usted	tiene un problema	El	tiene "que"	llevarle a casa
(They) Ellos tienen	**She**	**has a headache**	**We**	**have**	**to see you**
(it) Eso tiene	Ella	tiene un dolor de cabeza	Nosotros	tenemos "que"	verle
	You	**have a visitor**	**He**	**has**	**to live now**
	Usted	tiene un visitante	Ella	se tiene "que"	ir ahora

The 2nd Trigger Verb is "To Have"
It has two meanings in Spanish: "Tener" (tehnehr) o "Haber" (ahbehr)

Let us now review the Verb "Haber" (Ahbehr) in Spanish
The Verb "Haber" in Spanish is an auxiliary verb to Past Participle Verbs
Most Past Participle Verbs in Spanish end in "ido" or "ado"

To Have   Examples using Haber (ahbehr)

Haber (ahbehr)

(I)	Yo **he** (eh)
(You)	Usted **ha** (ah)
(He)	El **ha** (ah)
(She)	Ella **ha** (ah)
(We)	Nosotros **hemos**
(They)	Ellos **han**
(It)	Eso/Esto **ha** (ah)

I	**have**	**gotten mail today**
Yo	he	recibido correo hoy
You	**have**	**taken a long time**
Usted	ha	tomado mucho tiempo
She	**has**	**slept in the morning**
Ella	ha	dormido en la mañana
They	**have**	**studied all day**
Ellos	han	estudiado todo el día
They	**have**	**cooked all morning**
Ellos	han	cocinado toda la mañana
He	**has**	**been running all afternoon**
El	ha	estado corriendo toda la tarde

I	**have**	**gone to eat**
Yo	he	ido a comer
You	**have**	**not called me**
Usted	no me ha	llamado
He	**has**	**come to see me**
El	ha	venido a verme
She	**has**	**taken me home**
Ella	me	ha llevado a casa
I	**have**	**not gone to sleep**
Yo	no me he	ido a dormir
They	**have not**	**watched TV**
Ellos	no han	mirado TV

Lesson 6: Part 3

Here are examples of the Verb "Haber" (ahbehr) in Spanish,
It is used as an auxiliary verb to speak in Past Participle

To Have: Haber

I have done	**They have studied**	**You have understood**
Yo he hecho	Ellos han estudiado	Usted ha entendido
I have gotten	**I have run**	**He has written**
Yo he recibido	Yo he corrido	El ha escrito
I have taken	**She has walked**	**I have healed**
Yo he llevado	Ella ha caminado	Yo me he curado
You have cooked	**They have called**	**You have improved**
Yo he cocinado	Ellos han llamado	Usted ha mejorado
He has waited	**I have spoken**	**They have thought**
El ha esperado	Yo he hablado	Ellos han pensado
She has gone	**I have bought it**	**You have brought it**
Ella ha ido	Yo lo he comprado	Usted lo ha traído
She has seen	**She has shopped**	**She has bathed**
Ella ha visto	Ella ha ido de compras	Ella se ha bañado

Tener	Tener que	Pasado Participio
I have a great family Yo tengo una gran familia	**I have to see you tomorrow** Yo tengo que verle mañana	**I have received mail today** Yo he recibido correo hoy
I have a headache Yo tengo dolor de cabeza	**I have to come to see you** Yo tengo que venir a verle	**I have slept well yesterday night** Yo he dormido bien anoche
You have four good kids Usted tiene cuatro hijos buenos	**You have to go to eat** Usted tiene que ir a comer	**Yo have not done your work** Usted no ha hecho su trabajo
I have a good job Yo tengo un buen trabajo	**I have to meet with him today** Yo tengo que reunirme con el hoy	**I have seen her early today** Yo la he visto hoy temprano
He has problems with her El tiene problemas con ella	**He has to bring him the food** El tiene que traerle la comida	**He has made a big mistake** El ha cometido un gran error
They have a great life Ellos tienen una gran vida	**They have to hurry up** Ellos se tienen que apurar	**They have eaten a lot today** Ellos han comido mucho hoy
You have a lot of luck Ustedes tiene mucha suerte	**You have to finish the project** Usted tiene que terminar el proyecto	**We have sent her to school** Nosotros la hemos enviado a la escuela
I have a rough road ahead Yo tengo un camino difícil por delante	**We have to start moving** Nosotros tenemos que comenzar a movernos	**You have been absent lately** Ustedes han estado ausentes ultimamente
You have a lot of luck Ustedes tiene mucha suerte	**She has to pay attention** Ella tiene que poner atención	**She has bought new clothes** Ella ha comprado ropa nueva
She has a brand new car Ella tiene un coche nuevo	**It has to be fixed** Tiene que ser reparado	**It has been repaired already** Ya ha sido reparado
It has a broken light Tiene una luz rota	**I have to start all over again** Yo tengo que empezar de nuevo	**I have been thinking about it** Yo he estado pensando en ello

**3rd . Trigger Verb "To Want" is used in Spanish
to Express either Desire or To Give an order:**

Let us now review the Verb "Querer" (Kehrehr) in Spanish, it has two forms:
1) The Verb "Querer" in Spanish is used to express a desire or a wish
2) The Verb "Querer Que (Keh)" is used to express a command, request or order.

To Want	Examples	
Querer (Kehrehr)	**To express a desire**	**To give an order**
(I) Yo quiero (kee-eh-roh)	**I want to go to sleep**	**I want you to go to eat**
(You) Usted quiere (kee-eh-reh).	Yo me quiero ir a dormir	Yo quiero que usted vaya comer
(He) El quiere (kee-eh-reh)	**I want to learn Spanish**	**He wants you to write to him**
(She) Ella quiere (kee-eh-reh)	Yo quiero aprender español	El quiere que usted le escriba
(We) Nosotros queremos	**She wants to cook for you**	**We want you to think about it**
(You) Ustedes quieren	Ella quiere cocinarle a ustedes	Queremos que lo piense
(They) Ellos quieren	**They want to take you home**	**I want you to bring me the check**
(It) Eso/Esto quiere	Ellos quieren llevarle a casa	Yo quiero que me traiga la cuenta

Lesson 7: Part 1

Querer (kehrehr)		Querer Que (kehrehr)
Desire / Wish **Desear/Querer**	<u>Examples</u>	**Command / Order** **Comando/Orden**
I want to take you to the movies Yo quiero llevarle al cine		**I want that you stop calling me** Yo quiero que usted pare de llamarme
I want to go shopping today after lunch Yo quiero ir de compras hoy después de comer		**I want that you think about it carefully** Yo quiero que lo piense con cuidado
You want me to bring you anything? ¿Usted quiere que le traiga alguna cosa?		**Do you want that we get him ready?** ¿Usted quiere que lo tengamos listo?
He wants to buy a brand new pair of shoes El quiere comprar un par de zapatos nuevos		**He wants that you cal l h i m today at 2 p.m.** El quiere que usted lo llame hoy a las 2 p.m.
She wants to try to find a new job Ella quiere tratar de conseguir un trabajo nuevo		**She wants me n o t to bother her anymore** Ella quiere que yo no la moleste más

The 4th Trigger Verb "Can" is used in Spanish to express "Being Able To"
In Spanish means "Poder" (Pohdehr)

Poder (Pohdehr)	Examples:	Examples:
Yo puedo (poo-ehdoh)	**I can see you later**	**He can come at noon**
Usted puede (poo-ehde)	Yo puedo verle luego	El puede venir al mediodía
El puede (poo-ehde)	**She can go to see him**	**You can do it**
Elle puede (poo-ehde)	Ella puede ir a verle	Usted puede hacerlo
Nosotros podemos	**They can take you home**	**You can come in**
Ustedes pueden	Ellos pueden llevarle a casa	Usted puede entrar
Ellos pueden (poo-eden)	**He can come tomorrow**	**I can call you later**
Eso/Esto puede	El puede venir mañana	Yo puedo llamarle luego

Examples of verb Poder

I can come to see you this weekend
Yo puedo venir a verle éste fin de semana

I can call you every night at 8 p.m.
Yo puedo llamarle todas las noches a las 8 p.m.

He can take them to the park tomorrow at 4
El puede llevarles al parque mañana a las 4

She can not eat chicken
Ella no puede comer pollo

We can work together to solve the problem
Nosotros podemos trabajar juntos para resolver el problema

He can prepare for the test this week
El puede prepararse para el examen esta semana

You can bring them over to spend the day here
Usted puede traerlos a pasar el día aquí

You can go to the movies with them
Usted puede ir al cine con ellos

You can call me after lunch
Usted puede llamarme después del almuerzo

They can complain all they want, it won't make a difference
Ellos pueden protestar todo lo que quieran pero no hará diferencia

Ok. Let's use the Nouns, The 4 Trigger Verbs, The Magic Words and additional Infinitive Verbs to build more phrases.

I	Yo	(yoh)
You	Usted	(uhstehd)
He	El	(ehl)
She	Ella	(eyah)
We	Nosotros	(Nohsohtros)
You	Ustedes	(Uhstehdehs)
They	Ellos	(eyohs)
It	Eso/Esto	(Esoh/Estoh)

The 4 Trigger Verbs

To Be	Ser	(sehr)
To Be	Estar	(ehstahr)
To Have	Tener	(tehnehr)
To Have	Haber	(ahbehr)
To Want	Querer	(kehrehr)
Can	Poder	(pohdehr)

I have to go to call her
Yo tengo que ir a llamarla

I want to take you to dinner
Yo quiero llevarle a cenar

He can wait for you at noon
El puede esperar por usted al mediodía

I have to go to take notes
Yo tengo que ir a tomar notas

I can go to see you tomorrow
Yo puedo ir a verle mañana

We can cook rather quickly
Nosotros podemos cocinar muy rápido

We have to wait for her
Nosotros tenemos que esperar por ella

I want to come to see you
Yo quiero venir a verle

You can go to sleep
Usted puede irse a dormir

She wants to cook for you
Ella quiere cocinarle

I have to run to go to see him
Yo tengo que correr para ir a verle

They can come to run tonight
Ellos pueden venir a correr esta noche

He has to call her soon
El tiene que llamarla pronto

Additional Trigger Verbs:

Examples

To Go	**ir** (ihr)	
To Come	**Venir** (vehneer)	
To Take	**Tomar** (tohmar)	
To Buy	**Comprar** (comprar)	
To Cook	**Cocinar** (cocinar)	
To Wait	**Esperar** (esperar)	
To Run	**Correr** (correr)	
To Watch	**Mirar** (mirahr)	
To See	**Ver** (Vehr)	
To Give	**Dar** (Dahr)	
To Get	**Recibir** (Receebir)	
To Get	**Obtener** (Obtener)	
To Walk	**Caminar** (Caminar)	
To Write	**Escribir** (Escribir)	
To Read	**Leer** (Lehehr)	

You have to come to see her
Usted tiene que venir a verla

You can come to watch TV later
Usted puede venir a ver TV luego

She wants you to call soon
Ella quiere que la llame pronto

He can read pretty well
El puede leer muy bien

They have to run today
Ellos tienen que correr hoy

She wants to run every morning
Ella quiere correr todas las mañanas

They can take you to the airport now
Ellos pueden llevarle al aeropuerto ahora

You can go to buy groceries at three
Nosotros podemos comprar comida a las tres

He has to get mail this week
El tiene que recibir correo esta semana

He has to go to get his ID
El tiene que ir a obtener su ID

He has to learn to write often
El tiene que aprender a escribir a menudo

Lesson 9: Part 3

Now, "Let's" build phrases with what we have learned

I have to be a good father
Yo tengo que ser un buen padre

I want to be fair
Yo quiero ser justo

I can be often late
Yo puedo estar tarde a menudo

You have to be persistent
Usted tiene que ser persistente

You want to be the best
Usted quiere ser el major

You can be the last to come in
Usted puede ser el último en venir

We have to be polite
Nosotros tenemos que ser educados

We want to be the best
Nosotros queremos ser los mejores

We can be of great help to you
Nosotros le podemos ser de gran ayuda

I have to be there on time
Yo tengo que estar allí a tiempo

I want to be present
Yo quiero estar presente

I can be there at two
Yo puedo estar allá a las dos

You have to be alert all the time
Usted tiene que estar alerta todo el tiempo

You want to be ahead of the curve
Usted quiere estar adelante de la curva

You can have a lot of trouble soon
Ustedes pueden tener muchos problemas pronto

We have to be waiting for him at the gate
Nosotros tenemos que estar esperándole en la Puerta

He can be available later
El puede estar disponible luego

He has to be patient
El tiene que ser paciente

He wants to be like his father
El quiere ser como su padre

He can be a very good team mate
El puede ser un gran miembro del equipo

We want to be ready for him
Nosotros queremos estar listos para él

We can be in the losing end
Nosotros podemos estar en el lado perdedor

He has to be devastated
El tiene que estar devastado

He wants to be permanently on vacations
El quiere estar de vacaciones permanentemente

The Infinitive Verbs/ The Four Trigger Verbs

Infinitive Verbs		To Be	To Want	To Have	Can	Will
Nouns		Ser/Estar	Querer	Tener/ Haber	Poder	Ir a
I	Yo	Soy--Estoy	Quiero	Tengo--He	Puedo	Voy a
You	Usted	Es--Esta	Quiere	Tiene--Ha	Puede	Va a
He	El	Es--Esta	Quiere	Tiene--Ha	Puede	Va a
She	Ella	Es--Esta	Quiere	Tiene--Ha	Puede	Va a
We	Nosotros	Somos-Estamos	Queremos	Tenemos-Hemos	Podemos	Vamos a
You	Ustedes	Son--Estan	Quieren	Tienen--Han	Pueden	Van a
They	Ellos	Son--Estan	Quieren	Tienen--Han	Pueden	Van a
It	Eso/Esto	Es--Esta	Quiere	Tiene-Ha	Puede	Van a

Learning Step 8

The 4 Templates

Enable you to be conversant in:
- Gerund (action),
- Past Participle ,
- Future

and

- Conditional tenses ,

while using only "Infinitive Verbs"

1. Gerundio/ Gerund (Acción):

ENGLISH: To be + Verbo termina "ing"
SPANISH: Estar + Verbo termina en "iendo" o "ando"

How to convert an:
-        English "Infinitive Verb" into Gerund
To Walk—Kill "To"—add "ing" Walking
-        Spanish "Infinitive Verb" into Gerundio
Caminar---Kill "R"—add "ando"—Caminando
Example: To Walk=Caminar (Infinitive verb)

I am walking to eat
Yo estoy caminando a comer

Lesson 10: Part 1

Gerund/Gerundio

<u>English</u> : To Be + Verb ending in **"ing"**
<u>Spanish</u> : Estar + V erb ending in **iendo** o **ando**

-In English we speak in Gerund when we refer to "<u>Action</u>."
-And we use the Verb "<u>To Be</u>" followed followed by a verb ending in <u>ing.</u>
-In Spanish is exactly the same, Hispanics use the verb "<u>Estar</u>" (To Be) followed by a verb ending in <u>iendo</u> or <u>ando.</u>
<u>Example:</u>
 To Call: I am calling you tonight
 Llamar: Yo estoy llamándole esta noche

So, bottom line: verb endings in <u>ing</u> in English end in either <u>iendo or ando</u> in Spanish.

How to convert an Infinitive Verb to Gerund:
 <u>In English</u> we do this:
 To Call----Calling (kill the "<u>To</u>" add "<u>ing</u>")
 <u>In Spanish</u> they do this:
 Llamar----Llamando (kill de "R" add "<u>ando</u>")

Lesson 10: Part 2

Examples: Gerund (action)

I am calling you now
Yo estoy llamándole ahora

They are calling him today
Ellos están llamándole hoy

They are calling tonight
Ellos están llamándole esta noche

I am studying all morning
Yo estoy estudiando toda la mañana

They are studying today
Ellos están estudiando hoy

She is studying now
Ella está estudiando ahora

I am waiting at the house
Yo estoy esperando en la casa

We are waiting for you
Ellos están esperando por usted

You are waiting in vain
Usted está esperando en vano

I am writing to you every week
Yo estoy escribiéndole cada semana

They are writing every other week
Ellos están escribiendo cada dos semanas

He is writing often
El está escribiendo a menudo

I am trying to visit you
Yo estoy tratando de visitarle

She is trying to visit us
Ella está tratando de visitarnos

They are trying to call
Ellos están tratando de llamar

I am learning to speak Spanish
Yo estoy aprendiendo a hablar
español

She is learning about the country
Ella está aprendiendo acerca
del país

He is learning the basic
El está aprendiendo lo básico

I am watching hispanic TV
Yo estoy viendo la TV en español

You are watching her grow
Usted está mirándola crecer

He is watching the game
El está mirando el juego

Infinitive Verbs:

To Call : Llamar   To Study :Estudiar   To Wait :Esperar   To Write: Escribir   To Try: Tratar
To Learn: Aprender   To Watch: Mirar

2. Participle/Participio (Past Participle)

ENGLISH: To Have + Participle Verb
SPANISH: Haber + Verb ending in "ido" or "ado"

How to Convert an "Infinitive Verb" in Spanish into a past Participle Verb:
- Use the verb "Haber" (To Have) conjugation.
- Kill "R" add ending either ido or ado

Yo   He
Usted   Ha
El   Ha
Ella   Ha
Nosotros (as Hemos)   + Spanish Verb ending
Ustedes   Han   in "ido" or "ado"
Ellos(as) Han
Eso/Esto   Ha

Example: To Wait=Esperar
(Infinitive verb)
I have been waiting for you
Yo he estado esperando por usted

English: To have = In Spanish: Haber.   Examples in Past participle:

+ **Yo he**	(eh)	**To take: I have taken her home**	**To wait: They have been waiting for you**
+ **Usted ha**	(ah)	Llevar : Yo la he llevado a casa	Esperar: Ellos han estado esperando por usted
+ **El ha**	(ah)	**To eat: He has eaten at 12**	**To wash: She has been washing all morning**
+ **Ella ha**	(ah)	Comer: El ha comido a las 12	Lavar: Ella ha estado lavando toda la mañana
+ **Nosotros hemos**		**To learn: They have learned to read**	**To ask: He has been asking for you**
+ **Usted ha**	(ahn)	Aprender: Ellos han aprendido a leer	Preguntar: El ha estado preguntando por usted
+ **Ellos han**	(ahn)	**To talk: She has talked to him**	**To cook: They have been cooking today**
+ **Eso/Esto ha**	(ah)	Hablar: Ella ha hablado con él	Cocinar: Ellos han estado cocinando hoy

To study: We have studied	**To walk: We have walked**
Estudiar: Nosotros hemos estudiado	Caminar: Nosotros hemos caminado
To get: They have gotten no mail	**To think: You have thought about it**
Recibir: Ellos no han recibido correo	Pensar : Usted ha pensado acerca de eso
To go: I have gone to see her	**To come: You have been coming every year**
Ir : Yo he ido a verla	Venir: Usted ha estado viniendo cada año
To bring: He has brought a friend	**To win: We have been winning more**
Traer: El ha traído una amiga	Ganar: Nosotros hemos estado ganando más
To listen: She has listened to him	**To buy: I have been buying lots of vitamins**
Escuchar: Ella le ha escuchado	Comprar: Yo he estado comprando muchas vitaminas

For a list of Past Participle Verbs see Next Page.

Past Participle (Verbs)/(Verbos) Pasado Participle

Been *Sido*	**Been** *Estado*	**Arrived** *Llegado*	**Washed** *Lavado*	**Cooled** *Enfriado*	**Packed** *Empacado*	**Written** *Escrito*	**Fought** *Peleado*
Come *Venido*	**Talked** *Hablado*	**Calculated** *Calculado*	**Explained** *Explicado*	**Looked** *Mirado*	**Brought** *Traído*	**Replied** *Respondido*	**Thought** *Pensado*
Gotten *Recibido*	**Taken** *Lleva do/ Tomado*	**Seen** *Visto*	**Repeated** *Repetido*	**Appealed** *Apelado*	**Needed** *Necesitado*	**Heated** *Calentado*	**Watched** *Mirado*
Ran *Corrido*	**Cleaned** *Limpiado*	**Called** *Llamado*	**Had** *Tenido*	**Finished** *Finalizado*	**Disputed** *Disputado*	**Cooked** *Cocinado*	**Replied** *Respondido*
Done *Hecho*	**Failed** *Fallado*	**Given** *Dado*	**Listened** *Escuchado*	**Accepted** *Aceptado*	**Built** *Construído*	**Traveled** *Viajado*	**Grabbed** *Agarrado*
Wished *Deseado*	**Made** *Hecho*	**Walked** *Caminado*	**Bought** *Comprado*	**Asked** *Preguntado*	**Wanted** *Querido*	**Realized** *Dado cuenta*	**Started** *Empezado*
Remembered *Recordado*	**Baked** *Horneado*	**Put** *Puesto*	**Sat** *Sentado*	**Read** *Leído*	**Eaten** *Comido*	**Gone** *Ido*	**Enjoyed** *Disfrutado*
Fried *Frito*	**Heard** *Escuchado*	**Lost** *Perdido*	**Liked** *Gustado*	**Stood** *Parado*	**Bathed** *Bañado*	**Said** *Dicho*	**Searched** *Buscado*
Slept *Dormido*	**Agreed** *Acordado*	**Exited** *Salido*	**Left** *Dejado*	**Loved** *Amado*	**Woken** *Despertado*	**Layed** *Dejado*	**Saddened** *Entristecido*
Questioned *Preguntado*	**Entered** *Introducido*	**Hurt** *Herido*	**Found** *Encontrado*	**Flown** *Volado*	**Won** *Ganado*	**Cried** *Llorado*	**Shipped** *Enviado*
Ordered *Ordenado*	**Boiled** *Hervido*	**Dreamed** *Soñado*	**Drank** *Bebido*	**Paid** *Pagado*	**Swam** *Nadado*	**Waited** *Esperado*	**Started** *Empezado*
Answered *Respondido*	**Understood** *Entendido*	**Argued** *Discutido*	**Jumped** *Saltado*	**Forgotten** *Olvidado*	**Arrived** *Llegado*	**Dried** *Secado*	**Shown** *Mostrado*

3. Future/ Futuro

ENGLISH: Will + I nfinitiv e Verb.
SPANISH: Yo voy a + Infinitive Verb.

I will	Yo voy a
You will	Usted va a
He will	El va a
She will	Ella va a
We will	Nosotros vamos a
You will	Ustedes van a
They will	Ellos van a
It will	Eso/Esto va a

Example: To go = Ir To eat = Comer (Infinitive Verbs)
    I will go   to eat later
    Yo voy a ir   a comer después

Lesson 12: Part 1

Examples

ENGLISH: Will + Infinitive Verb.
SPANISH: Yo voy a + Infinitive Verb.

I will = Yo voy a You will = Usted va a He will = El va a She will = Ella va a We will = Nosotros vamos a You will = Ustedes van a They will = Ellos van a It will = Eso/Esto va a	**I will go to run later** Yo voy a ir a corer después **You will not finish** Usted no va a terminar **She will call you later** Ella le va a llamarle luego **You will take me home** Usted va a llevarme a casa **He will wait for you at 12** El le va a esperar a las doce **He will bring you lunch at 1** El le va a traer el almuerzo a la 1	**They will go to visit you soon** Ellos van a venir a visitarle pronto **I will study all day** Yo voy a estudiar todo el día **They will get your food** Ellos van a traerle la comida **He will cook for you today** El va a cocinarle hoy **He will fly out at 3** El va a volar a las 3 **You will not be on time** Usted no va a estar a tiempo

4. Conditional/ Condicional

What is a conditional verb?

Any verb that depicts a condition ; In English any verb that ends in "ould", in Spanish any verb that ends in "ia" o "iera" are conditional verbs.

How to convert a Spanish Verb into a Conditional tense Verb?

By adding the ending "ia" to any infinitive verb (Note: as previously explained, in Spanish all infinitive verbs end in "R".

ENGLISH: Could
          Should   } — + Verbo inf initivo
          Would

SPANISH: <u>Verbo in initivo + "ia" o "iera"</u>

Example: <u>To go</u> = Ir
<u>To run</u> = Correr
I would go to run if you would come with me
Yo iría correr si usted viniera conmigo

Lesson 13: Part 1

EXAMPLES:

He would try to finish tomorrow if he gets paid
El trataría de terminar mañana si recibe el pago
I could go to run if the weather is nice
Yo podría ir a correr si el clima está agradable
You should come to study only if you are ready for it
Usted debería venir a estudiar sólo si usted está listo para ello
I would go to visit you if you would be available for me
Yo iría a visitarle si usted estuviera disponible para mí
We would eat at your place if you would cook for all of us
Nosotros comeríamos en su casa si ustedes cocinaran para todos nosotros
They would call you at noon if you co uld have an answer for them
Ellos llamarían al mediodía si usted tuviera una respuesta para ellos
I would take you to the airport if you are ready by 8
Yo le llevaría al aeropuerto si usted estuviera listo a las 8
You would be very happy if you co uld just try to lend a hand Usted
se sentiría muy contento si simplemente tratara de dar una mano
She would wait for them at noon if they are all showing up
Ella esperaría por ellos al mediodía si todos ellos vienen
They would preffer if you don't do anything for the moment
Ellos preferirían que usted no haga nada por el momento

English: Conditional	Español Condicional
Could	Podría
Should	Debería
Would eat	Comería
Would call	Llamaría
Would wait	Esperaría
Would talk	Hablaría
Would study	Estudiaría
Would buy	Compraría
Would take	Llevaría

Infinitive V.

Can	Poder
Shall	Deber
To go	Ir
To eat	Comer
To call	Llamar
To wait	Esperar
To talk	Hablar
To study	Estudiar
To buy	Comprar
To take	Llevar

"The Four Templates"

Through this method you'll build any phrase with an "Infinitive Verb"
Using the same verbs, l et us build some sentences using the four templates

Gerund/ Gerundio (Action)

To eat = Comer; Kill the "r" & add "iendo"
Yo estoy comiendo
I   am   eating

To walk = Caminar; kill the "r" & add "ando"
El esta caminando
He is   walking

Particip le/Particip io

To eat = Comer; kill the
Yo he comido
I have eaten   "r" & add "ido"

To walk = Caminar; kill
El ha caminado
He has walked   the "r" & add "ado"

Future/ Futuro

To eat = Comer; Infinitive Verb does not change
Yo voy a comer
I   will   eat

To walk = Caminar; Infinitive Verb does not change
El va a caminar
He will   walk

Conditional/Condicional

Yo comeria
I   would eat   To eat = Comer; Add "ia"
                        to Infinitive Verb

El   caminaria
He would walk

                        To walk = Caminar; Add
                        "ia" to Infinitive Verb

Learning Step 9

The 11 Verbs

We revisit English grammar in order to translate properly from English to Spanish

Pay close attention to these 11 verbs because you need proper English to speak proper Spanish!

To be	Ser/estar	To have	Haber	Can	Poder
Could	Podría	**Shall**	Deber	**Should**	Debería
Will	Ir a	**Must**	Deber	**Might**	Poder
May	Podría	**Would**	Habria/Hubiera		

These verbs have unique features that we need to be mindful of:

1)   If any other verb follows one of these 11 verbs, there is never a "To" after it.

Examples : In English most of the times a "To" follows a 1st. verb: I have to go – I want to go – I like to go. Not on these 11 verbs: I am going – I can go – I could go – I may go – I will go.

2)   Except for the verbs To Be & To Have the infinitive form of the other 9 verbs is w/o a "To."

Example : Can, May, Shall always start w/o a "To".

3)   When asking a question with these 11 verbs, we don't use "Do" or "Did" at the beginning of the question; simply flip the verb & the noun (which is the only way Hispanics do it).

Example : Normally is: Do I want?-Did I have?, But with these 11 verbs we just flip":Am I?-Can I?

4)   When Negating with these 11 verbs, we don't use "Don't" or "Didn't" we simply add "not" after the verb.

Example : Normally is: I don't want – I don't have to. But with these Verbs we negate as follows: I am not coming, You can not go, You have not eaten.

5)   Except for To Be & To Have, these verbs have no conjugations.

Example : I can-He can / I may- He may / we must-they must

Learning Step 10

Questions & Negations

As you'll see both questions and negations are far easier in Spanish than in English

Lesson 15

In Spanish, <u>Questions are always and only formulated by flipping</u> the noun and the verb

Examples:

<u>**Usted quiere**</u> ir a comer
<u>**¿Quiere usted**</u> ir a comer?
(Do you want to go to eat?)

<u>**Usted tiene**</u> que venir
<u>**¿Tiene usted**</u> que venir?
(Do you have to come?)

<u>**Yo puedo ir**</u> a visitarla
<u>**¿Puedo yo ir**</u> a visitarla?
(Can I go to visit her?)

<u>**Ella debería**</u> llamarme
<u>**¿Debería ella**</u> llamarme?
(Should she call me?)

In Spanish, Negations are <u>always and only formulated by inserting a No (Noh) right after the noun.</u>

Examples:

<u>**Usted quiere**</u> ir a comer
<u>**Usted no quiere**</u> ir a comer
(You do not want to go to eat)

<u>**Usted tiene**</u> que venir
<u>**Usted no tiene**</u> que venir
(You don´t have to come)

<u>**Yo puedo**</u> ir a vistarla
<u>**Yo no puedo**</u> ir a visitarla
(I can not go to visit her)

<u>**Ella debería**</u> llamarme
<u>**Ella no debería**</u> llamarme
(She should not call me)

"There is"

These two words are expressed in Spanish through one word:

"HAY" (AEE)

Lesson 16

There is: Hay **(ah-ee)**

There is: Hay (singular)
There are: Hay (plural)
There was: Hubo (singular)
There were: Hubo (plural)
There has been: Ha habido
There have been: Han habido
There will be: Va a haber
There would be: Habría o hubiera
There would have been: Hubieran habido

Learning Step 12

"Er-Est-Y"

Learn how these endings are expressed in Spanish

Practice them, especially the conjugations!

The Endings Er - Est - Y

Shorter	Más corto	**Shortest**	Lo más corto		
Better	Mejor	**Best**	Lo mejor		
Taller	Más alto	**Tallest**	Lo más alto		
Faster	Más rápido	**Fastest**	Lo más rápido	**Examples:**	
Quicker	Más rápido	**Quickest**	Lo más rápido		
Smaller	Más pequeño	**Smallest**	Lo más pequeño	**Shorter than** = Más corto que	
Slower	Más despacio	**Slowest**	Lo mas despacio	**Better than** = Mejor que (*)	
Hotter	Más caliente	**Hottest**	Lo más caliente	**Taller than** = Más alto que	
Colder	Más frío	**Coldest**	Lo más frío	**Faster than** = Más rápido que	
Dumber	Más tonto	**Dumbest**	Lo más tonto		
Fewer	Más poco	**Fewest**	Lo más poco		
Shorty	Cortito o Cortico	**As___ as**	Tan__como		
Tardy	Retardado	**More__than**	Más__que		
Weepy	Lloroso				

(*) Más y mejor are both superlatives , so they are never presented together

Lesson 17: Part 2

WHEN THE ENDING -ER- IS APPLIED TO AN INFINITIVE VERB
IT CONVERTS IT INTO A PERSON

To drive = manejar	Driver = conductor
To eat = comer	Eater = comilón/glotón
To play = jugar	Player = jugador
To run = correr	Runner = corredor
To sleep = dormir	Sleeper = dormilón
To write = escribir	Writer = escritor
To read = leer	Reader = lector
To pay = pagar	Payer = pagador
To wash = lavar	Washer = lavadora
To speak = hablar	Speaker = hablador

Learning Step 13

The Verb:

To Have

Learn the different grammar rules that apply to it

Practice them, specially the pronunciations!

The strange case of the verb To Have

In English depending on the context, there are three uses and different grammar rules for the verb
"To have" :

1) **Ownerswhi or Posession.** Examples: I have a headache / Yo tengo un dolor de cabeza.

I have a son / Yo tengo un hijo.

2) **Duty or Responsibility**. Examples : I have to go / Yo me tengo que ir.

You have to come / Usted tiene que venir.

3) **Past Participle**. (already happned) Examples: I have done it! / ¡Ya lo he hecho!

In Spanish the verb **"to have"** se expresa de la siguiente manera:

Tener	Tener que	Haber
Hold/ ownership	**Duty/ responsibility**	**(Already happened)**
I have a family	I have to go to eat	I have gone to eat early
Yo tengo una familia	Yo tengo que ir a comer	Yo he ido a comer temprano

Learning Step 14

The Verb:

To Like

Learn the different grammar rules that apply to it

Practice them, specially the pronunciations!

"The Even Stranger Case of the Verb To Like"

Verb "GUSTAR/DISFRUTAR"

To Like

"Like/Enjoy To" (Present)				"Would Like/Enjoy To" (Conditional)			infinitive verb
A	Mí	Me	-	Gusta	A	Mí	Me	-	Gustaria
A	Usted	Le	-	Gusta	A	Usted	Le	-	Gustaria
A	Él	Le	-	Gusta	A	El	Le	-	Gustaria
A	Ella	Le	-	Gusta	A	Ella	Le	-	Gustaria
A	Nosotros	Nos	-	Gusta	A	Nosotros	Nos	-	Gustaria
A	Ustedes	Les	-	Gusta	A	Ustedes	Les	-	Gustaria
A	Ellos Ellas	Les	-	Gusta	A	Ellos Ellas	Les	-	Gustaria
A	Eso/Esto	Le	-	Gusta	A	Eso/Esto	Les	-	Gustaria

"The Even Stranger Case of the Verb To Like"

Verb "GUSTAR/DISFRUTAR"

To Like

"Like/Enjoy To" (Past Participle)				"Will Like/Enjoy To" (Future)				infinitive verb
A	Mí	Me	Ha	Gustado	A	Mí	Me	Va a	Gustar
A	Usted	Le	Ha	Gustado	A	Usted	Le	Va a	Gustar
A	Él	Le	Ha	Gustado	A	El	Le	Va a	Gustar
A	Ella	Le	Ha	Gustado	A	Ella	Le	Va a	Gustar
A	Nosotros	Nos	Ha	Gustado	A	Nosotros	Nos	Va a	Gustar
A	Ustedes	Les	Ha	Gustado	A	Ustedes	Les	Va a	Gustar
A	Ellos Ellas	Les	Ha	Gustado	A	Ellos Ellas	Les	Va a	Gustar
A	Eso/Esto	Le	Ha	Gustado	A	Eso/Esto	Les	Va a	Gustar

"Have Been Liking/Enjoying" (Participle)				(Gerund)	
A	Mí	Me	Ha	Estado	Gustando
A	Mí	Me	Ha	Estado	Gustando
A	Mí	Me	Ha	Estado	Gustando
A	Mí	Me	Ha	Estado	Gustando
A	Mí	Me	Ha	Estado	Gustando
A	Mí	Me	Ha	Estado	Gustando
A	Mí	Me	Ha	Estado	Gustando
A	Mí	Me	Ha	Estado	Gustando

"The Even Stranger Case of the Verb To Like"

Verb "GUSTAR/DISFRUTAR"

To Like

In Spanish the verb "To Like" is preceeded by a reflexive instead of a noun, the noun is replaced by a reflexive & the verb.

"Gustar" is always conjugated in 3rd person (Gusta). There are 2 ways to express the verb "To Like."

This is wrong	1st.Choice, " Abbreviated "	2nd. Choice, " Long Version "
Yo gusto	Me Gusta	A Mí Me Gusta
Usted Gusta	Le Gusta	A Usted Le Gusta
El Gusta	Le Gusta	A El Le Gusta
Ella Gusta	Le Gusta	A Ella Le Gusta
Nosotros Gustamos	Nos Gusta	A Nosotros Nos Gusta
Ustedes Gustan	Les Gusta	A Ustedes Les Gusta
Ellos Gustan	Les Gusta	A Ellos Les Gusta
Eso/Esto Gusta	Le Gusta	A Eso/Esto Les Gusta

¿Qué va a pasar?	¿Qué le pasa a usted?	A mí me pasa
What will happen?	What happens to you?	It happens to me
¿Qué va a traer?	¿Qué le pasaría a usted si…?	A mí me pasaría
What will you bring?	What would happen to you if	It would happen to me
¿Quién le va a traer?	¿Qué le ha pasado a usted..?	A mí me ha pasado
Who will bring you?	What has happened to you?	It has happened to me
¿Quién le va a buscar?	¿Qué le va a pasar a usted?	A mí me va a pasar
Who will pick you up?	What will happen to you?	It will happen to me
¿Quién le va a encontrar?	¿Qué le ha estado pasando?	A mí me ha estado pasando
Who will find you?	What has been happening to you?	It has been happening to me
¿Quién le va a cortar el pelo?	¿Quién le va a lavar el carro?	A mí me duele la cabeza
Who will cut your hair?	Who will wash your car?	I have a headache
A mí me parece demasiado	A mí me trae de vuelta	A mí me lleva mi esposa
It seems too much for me	Bring me back	My wife takes me
A mí me compra unos zapatos	A mí me trae una copa de vino	A mí me falló usted
Buy me a pair of shoes	I will like a cup of wine	You've failed me
A mí no me cabe en la cabeza	A mí se me extravió el carro	A mí se me perdió la cartera
It does not get through my head	I've lost my car	I've lost my purse
A mí se me olvidó llamarle	A mí no me caen nada bien	A mí no me habla ella
I forgot to call you	I do not like them at all	She does not talk to me

Learning Step 15

A Mi Me & Me

Learn the different grammar rules that apply to it

"This Construction can be used with any Spanish Verb in 3rd Person"

In English this way of talking starts with "it."

No Nouns :   Instead is spoken in either of this 2 ways:

-Yo	Me	+ Verb in 3rd Person	or	A Mí	Me	+ Verb in 3rd Person
-Usted	Le	+ Verb in 3rd Person	or	A Usted	Le	+ Verb in 3rd Person
-El	Le	+ Verb in 3rd Person	or	A El	Le	+ Verb in 3rd Person
-Ella	Le	+ Verb in 3rd Person	or	A Ella	Le	+ Verb in 3rd. Person
-Nosotros	Nos	+ Verb in 3rd Person	or	A Nosotros	Nos	+ Verb in 3rd. Person
-Ustedes	Les	+ Verb in 3rd Person	or	A Ustedes	Les	+ Verb in 3rd. Person
-Ellos	Les	+ Verb in 3rd Person	or	A Ustedes	Les	+ Verb in 3rd. Person
-Eso/Esto	Le	+ Verb in 3rd Person	or	A Ella	Le	+ Verb in 3rd. Person

Examples:

A mí me pesa	A usted le duele	A él le disgusta	A ella le entristece
it weights on you	it pains you	it disgusts him	it saddens her
A nosotros nos relaja	A ustedes les complace	A ellos les sorprende	A el le cuesta
it relaxes us	it pleases you	it surprises them	it is hard for him
A mí me preocupa	A mí me aburre	A mí me asusta	A mí me parece
It worries me	It bores me	It scares me	It seems to me
A usted le cuesta	A ellos les intriga	A nosotros nos aturde	A ella le afecta
It costs you	It intrigues them	It stuns us	It affects her

Following is a list of verbs in 3rd Person to practice "A Mi Me"

List of Verbs conjugated in 3rd Person

Parece	Mata	Manipula	Traumatiza	Lleva	Afecta
Seems	Kills	Manipulates	Traumatizes	Takes	Affects
Nace	Convence	Falla	Descontrola	Atrae	Hace
Borns	Convences	Fails	Loses Control	Attracts	Makes
Cabe	Tarda	Fascina	Acaba	Toma	Intimida
Fits	Delays	Fascinates	Finishes	Takes	Intimidates
Basta	Pierde	Habla	Llega	Detiene	Encanta
Suffices	Loses	Talks	Gets/Arrives	Stops	Enchants
Preocupa	Detiene	Simpatiza	Pasa	Preocupa	Duele
Worries	Detains	Sympathizes	Happens	Worries	Pains
Relaja	Intriga	Cae	Enerva	Maravilla	Trae
Relaxes	Intrigues	Falls	Enervates	Marvels	Brings
Cansa	Causa	Resbala	Lava	Aburre	Irrita
Tires	Causes	Skeeds	Washes	Bores	Irritates
Gana	Sabe	Olvida	Invita	Gana	Duerme
Wins	Knows	Forgets	Invites	Wins	Sleeps
Alegra	Mortifica	Motiva	Avergüenza	Cuesta	Corta
Make Happy	Mortifies	Motivates	Embarrasses	Costs	Cuts
Aturde	Asombra	Asusta	Motiva	Entretiene	Angustia
Stuns	Surprises	Scares	Motivates	Entertains	Anguish
Honra	Harta	Ilusiona	Enorgullece	Mata	Resbala
Honors	Satiates	Illusions	Prides	Kills	Skates
Choca	Impresiona	Afecta	Tiene	Quiere	Odia
Shocks	Shocks	Affects	Has	Want	Hates

Learning Step 16

The Expression

"Acabo De"

(just done/just finished/just completed "it")

Lesson 21

English:

I have just	+ past particip le verb
You have just	+ past participle verb
He has just	+ past participle verb
She has just	+ past participle verb
We have just	+ past participle verb
You have just	+ past participle verb
They have just	+ past participle verb
It has just	+ past participle verb

Spanish :

Yo me acabo de	+ infinitiv e verb
Usted se acaba de	+ infinitive verb
El se acaba de	+ infinitive verb
Ella se acaba de	+ infinitive verb
Nosotros nos acabamos de	+ infinitive verb
Ustedes se acaban de	+ infinitive verb
Ellos se acaban de	+ infinitive verb
Eso/Esto se acaba de	+ infinitive verb

Examples:

(Yo) acabo de comer
I have just eaten

(Yo) Me acabo de levantar
I have just woken up

(El) acaba de llamar por teléfono
He has just phoned us

(Ellos) acaban de regresar de compras
They have just come back from shopping

(Ustedes) acaban de cometer un error
You have just committed (made) an error

(Usted) acaba de determinar su turno
You have just finished your shift

(Nosotros) Nos acabamos de ir
We have just left

(Ella) acaba de llevarle al colegio
She has just taken him to school

(Yo) Me acabo de recordar de la cita
I have just remembered the appointment

(Usted) Se acaba de perder la película
You have just missed the movie

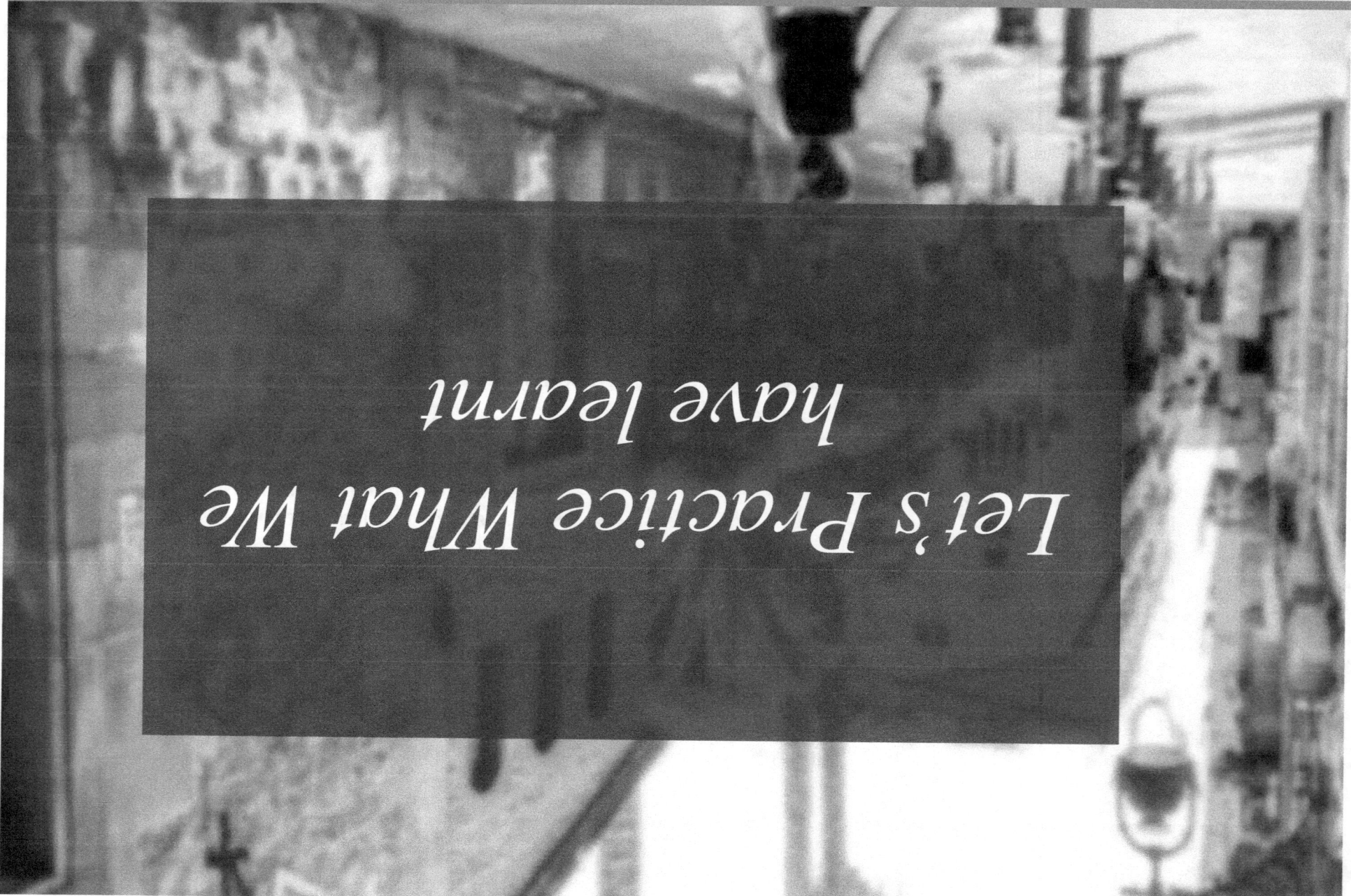

Let's Practice What We
have learnt

Infinitives

Example: <u>To Cook</u> (Infinitive Verb) Cocinar

The Four Templates

Present	Gerund	Future	Past Particip le	Conditional
I cook	I am cooking	I will cook	I have cooked	I would cook
Yo cocino	Yo estoy cocinando	Yo voy a cocinar	Yo he cocinado	Yo cocinaría

I will be cooking
Yo voy a estar cocinando

I was cooking
Yo estaba cocinando

I have to cook
Yo tengo que cocinar

I have been cooking
Yo he estado cocinando

I would have cooked
Yo hubiera cocinado

I did cook
Yo cociné

Example:To <u>Wait</u> (Infinitive Verb) Esperar

The Four Templates

Present	Gerund	Future	Past Particip le	Conditional
I wait	I am waiting	I will wait	I have waited	I would wait
Yo espero	Yo estoy esperando	Yo voy a esperar	Yo he esperado	Yo esperaría

I will be waiting
Yo voy a estar esperando

I have to wait
Yo tengo que esperar

I have been waiting
Yo he estado esperando

I would have waited
Yo hubiera esperado

Infinitives (Translate)

Examples: Correr (Infinitive Verb) <u>To run</u>   The Four Templates

Present	Gerund	Future	Past Particip le	Conditional
I run	I am runnning	I will run	I have run	I would run

I will be running	I was running	I have to run		I have been running
I would have run	I ran			

Examples: Comer (Infinitive Verb) <u>To eat</u>   The Four Templates

Present	Gerund	Future	Past Participle	Conditional
I eat	I am eating	I will eat	I have eaten	I would eat

I will be eating	I was eating	I have to eat		I have been eating
I would have eaten	I ate			

Infinitives (Translate)

Examples: Hablar (In finitive Verb) To talk

The Four Templates

Present	Gerund	Future	Past Participle	Conditional
I talk	I am talking	I will talk	I have talked	I would talk

I will be talking	I was talking	I have to talk	I have been talking

I would have spoken   I spoke

Exampl es: Llamar (Infinitive Verb) To call

The Four Templates

Present	Gerund	Future	Past Participle	Conditional
Yo llamo	I am calling	I will call	I have called	I would call

I will be calling	I was calling	I have to call	I have been calling

I would have called   I called

Infinitives (Translate)

Present	Gerund	Future	Past Participle	Conditional
I take	I m taking	I will take	I have taken	I would take

I will be taking	I was taking	I have to take	I have been taking	
I would have taken	I took			

Examples: Recibir (Infinitive Verb) <u>To get</u>   The Four Templates

Present	Gerund	Future	Past Participle	Conditional
I get	I am getting	I will get	I have gotten	I would get

I will be getting	I was getting	I have to get	I have been getting	
I would have gotten	I got			

Infinitives (Translate)

Examples: Pensar (Infinitive Verb) <u>To think</u>   The Four Templates

Present	Gerund	Future	Past Participle	Conditional
I think	I am thinking	I will think	I have thought	I would think

I will be thinking	I was thinking		I have to think	I have been thinking
I would have thought	I thought			

Examples: Estudiar (Infinitive Verb) <u>To study</u>   The Four Templates

Present	Gerund	Future	Past Participle	Conditional
I get	I am getting	I will get	I have gotten	I would get

I will be studying	I was studying		I have to study	I have been studying
I would have studied	I studied			

Infinitives (Translate)

Examples: Escribir (In finitive Verb) <u>To write</u>　　　　　　　　　　**The Four Templates**

Present	Gerund	Future	Past Participle	Conditional
I write	I am writing	I will write	I have written	I would write

I will be writing　　　　　　I was writing　　　　　　I have to write　　　　I have been writing

I would have written　　　　I wrote

Examples: Leer (Infinitive Verb) <u>To read</u>　　　　　　　　　　**The Four Templates**

Present	Gerund	Futuro	Pasado Participio	Condicional
I read	I am reading	I will read	I have read	I would read

I will be reading　　　　　　I was reading　　　　　I have to read　　　　I have been reading

I would have read　　　　　I read

Infinitives (Translate)

Ejemplos: Hacer (Infinitive Verb) <u>To Do</u>   The Four Templates

Present	Gerund	Fu ture	Past Particip le	Conditional
I do	I am doing	I will do	I have done	I would do

I will be doing	I was doing		I have to do	I have been doing
I would have done	I did			

E xampl es: Trabajar (Infinitive Verb) <u>To Work</u>   The Four Templates

Present	Gerund	Future	Past Particip le	Conditional
I work	I am working	I will work	I have worked	I would work

I will be working	I was working		I have to work	I have been working
I would have worked	I worked			

Negation

Examples: <u>To Cook</u> (Infinitive Verb) Cocinar   The Four Templates

Present	Gerund	Future	Past Participle	Conditional
I don't cook	I am not cooking	I won't cook	I haven't cooked	I wouldn't cook
Yo no cocino	Yo no estoy cocinando	Yo no voy a cocinar	Yo no he cocinado	Yo no cocinaría

I won't be cooking   I wasn't cooking   I don't have to cook   I haven't been cooking
Yo no voy a estar cocinando   Yo no estaba cocinando   Yo no tengo que cocinar   Yo no he estado cocinando
I wouldn't have cooked   I didn't cook
Yo no hubiera cocinado   Yo no cociné

Examples: <u>To Wait</u> (Infinitive Verb) Esperar   The Four Templates

Present	Gerund	Future	Past Participle	Conditional
I don't wait	I am not waiting	I won't wait	I haven't wait ed	I wouldn't wait
Yo no espero	Yo no estoy esperando	Yo no voy a esperar	Yo no he esperado	Yo no esperaría

I won't be waiting   I wasn't waiting   I don't have to wait
Yo no voy a estar esperando   Yo no estaba esperando   Yo no tengo que esperar
I would not have waited   I did not wait
Yo no hubiera esperado   Yo no esperé

I haven't been waiting
Yo no he estado esperando

Negation (Translate)

Examples: Correr (Infinitive Verb) <u>To Run</u>

The Four Templates

Present	Gerund	Future	Past Participle	Conditional
I don't run	I am not running	I won't run	I haven't run	I wouldn't run
I won't be running	I wasn't running	I don't have to run		I haven't been running
I wouldn't have run	I didn't run			

Examples: Comer (Infinitive Verb) <u>To Eat</u>

The Four Templates

Present	Gerund	Futuro	Past Participle	Conditional
I don't eat	I am not eating	I won't eat	I haven't eaten	I wouldn't eat
I wouldn't be eating	I wasn't eating	I don't have to eat		I haven't been eating
I wouldn't have eaten	I didn't eat			

Negation (Translate)

Examples: Hablar (Infinitive Verb) <u>To Talk</u>   The Four Templates

Present	Gerund	Future	Past Participle	Conditional
I don't talk	I am not talking	I won' t talk	I haven' t spoken	I wouldn't talk
I won't be talking Y	I wasn't talking		I don't have to talk	I haven't been talking
I wouldn't have spoken	I didn't talk			

Examples: Llamar (Infinitive Verb) <u>To Call</u>   The Four Templates

Present	Gerund	Future	Past Participle	Conditional
I don't call	I am not calling	I won't call	I haven't called	I wouldn't call
I won't be calling	I wasn't calling		I don't have to call	I haven't been calling
I wouldn't have called	I didn't call			

Negation (Translate)

Examples: Llevar (Infinitive Verb) To Take

The Four Templates

Present	Gerund	Future	Past Participle	Conditional
I don't take	I am not taking	I won't take	I haven't taken	I wouldn't take
I won't be taking	I wasn't taking		I don't have to take	I haven't been taking
I wouldn't have taken	I didn't take			

Examples: Recibir (Infinitive Verb) To Get

The Four Templates

Present	Gerund	Future	Past Participle	Conditional
I don't get	I am not getting	I won't get	I haven't gotten	I wouldn't get
I wouldn't be getting	I wasn't getting		I don't have to get	I haven't been getting
I wouldn't have gotten	I didn't get			

Negation (Translate)

Examples: Pensar (Infinitive Verb) <u>To Think</u>   The Four Templates

Present	Gerund	Future	Past Participle	Conditional
I don't think	I am not thinking	I wont think	I haven't thought	I wouldn't think

I won' t be thinking   I wasn't thinking   I don't have to think   I haven't been thinking

I wouldn't have been thinking   I didn't think

Examples: Estudiar (Infinitive Verb) <u>To Study</u>   The Four Templates

Present	Gerund	Future	Past Participle	Conditional
I don't study	I am not studying	I won't study	I haven't studied	I wouldn't study

I won't be studying   I wasn't studying

I wouldn't have studied   I didn't study   I don't have to study   I haven't been studying

Negation (Translate)

Exampl es: Escribir (Infinitive Verb) <u>To Write</u>

Present	Gerund	Future	Past Participle	Conditional
I don't write	I am not writing	I won't write	I haven't written	I wouldn't write

I won't be writing   I wasn't writing

I don't have to write   I haven't been writing

I wouldn't have written   I didn't write

Exampl es: Leer (Infinitive Verb) <u>To Read</u>

The Four Templates

Present	Gerund	Future	Past Participle	Conditional
I don't write	I am not writing	I won't write	I haven't written	I wouldn't write

I won't be reading   I wasn't reading

I don't have to read   I haven't been reading

I wouldn't have read   I didn't read

Negation (Translate)

Examples: Hacer (Infinitive Verb) To Do

The Four Templates

Present	Gerund	Future	Past Participle	Conditional
I don't do	I am not doing	I won't do	I haven't done	I wouldn't do

I won't be doing	I wasn't doing		I don't have to do	I haven't been doing
I wouldn't have done	I didn't do			

Examples: Trabajar (Infinitive Verb) To Work

The Four Templates

Present	Gerund	Future	Past Participle	Conditional
I don't work	**I am not working**	I won't work	I haven't worked	I wouldn't work

I won't be working	I wasn't working		I don't have to work	I haven't been working
I wouldn't have worked	I didn't work			

Questions

Example: To <u>Cook</u> (Infinitive Verb) Cocinar   The Four Templates

Present	Gerund	Future	Past Participle	Conditional
Do I cook?	Am I cooking?	Will I cook?	Have I cooked?	Would I cook?
¿Cocino yo?	¿Estoy yo cocinando?	¿Voy a cocinar yo?	¿He yo cocinado?	¿Cocinaría yo?

Will I be cooking?   Was I cooking?   Do I have to cook?   Have I been cooking?
¿Voy a estar cocinando yo?   ¿Estaba cocinando yo?   ¿Tengo yo que cocinar?   ¿He estado cocinando yo?
Would I have cooked?   Did I cook?
¿Hubiera yo cocinado?   ¿Cociné Yo?

Example: To <u>Wait</u> (Infinitive Verb) Esperar   The Four Templates

Present	Gerund	Future	Past Participle	Conditional
Do I wait?	Am I waiting?	Will I wait?	Have I waited?	Would I wait?
¿Espero yo?	¿Estoy yo esperando?	¿Voy yo a esperar?	¿He yo esperado?	¿Esperaría yo?

Will I be waiting?   Was I waiting?   Do I have to wait?   Have I been waiting?
¿Voy a estar esperando yo? ¿Estaba esperando yo? ¿Tengo que esperar yo? ¿He estado esperando yo?
Would I have waited?   Did I wait?
¿Hubiera esperado yo?   ¿Esperé yo?

Questions (Translate)

Example: Correr (Infinitive Verb) <u>To Run</u>   The Four Templates

Present	Gerund	Future	Past Participle	Conditional
Do I run?	Am I running?	Will I run?	Have I run?	Will I run?

Will I be running ?	Was I running?			
			Do I have to run?	Have I been running ?
Would I have run ?	Did I run?			

Example: Comer (Infinitive Verb) <u>To eat</u>   The Four Templates

Present	Gerund	Future	Past Participle	Conditional
Do I eat ?	Am I eating?	Will I eat ?	Have I eaten?	Would I eat ?

Will I be eating ?	Was I eating?			
			Do I have to eat?	Have I been eating ?
Would I have eaten? ?	Did I eat ?			

Questions (Translate)

Example: Hablar (Infinitive Verb) <u>To talk</u>   **The Four Templates**

Present	**Gerund**	**Future**	**Past Particip le**	**Conditional**
Do I talk ?	Am I talking?	Will I talk ?	Have I talked?	Would I talk ?

Will I be talking ?	Was I talking?		Do I have to talk? Have I been talking ?	
Would I have talked ?	Did I talk ?			

Example: Llamar (Infinitive Verb) <u>To call</u>   **The Four Templates**

Present	**Gerund**	**Future**	**Past Particip le**	**Conditional**
Do I call?	Am I calling?	Will I call?	Have I called ?	Would I call?

Will I be calling ?	Was I calling?		Did I have to call? Have I been calling ?	
Would I have called ?	Did I call?			

Questions (Translate)

Example: Llevar (Infinitive Verb) <u>To take</u>

The Four Templates

Present	Gerund	Future	Past Particip le	Conditional
Do I take?	Will I take?	Will I take?	Have I taken?	Would I take?

Will I be taking?   Was I taking?

Do I have to take? Have I been taking ?

Would I have taken ?   Did I take?

Example: Recibir (Infinitive Verb) <u>To get</u>

The Four Templates

Present	Gerund	Future	Past Particip le	Conditional
Do I get ?	Am I getting?	Will I get ?	Have I gotten?	Would I get ?

Have I been getting ?   Was I getting?

Do I have to get?   Have I been getting ?

Would Have I gotten ?   Did I receive ?

Questions (Translate)

Example: Pensar (Infinitive Verb) <u>To think</u>

The Four Templates

Present	Gerund	Future	Past Particip le	Conditional
Do I think ?	Am I thinking?	Will I think ?	Have I thought ?	Would I think ?

Will I be thinking ?   Was I thinking?

Do I have to think?   Have I been thinking ?

Would I have thouhgt ?   Did I ?

Example: Estudiar (Infinitive Verb) <u>To study</u>

The Four Templates

Present	Gerund	Future	Past Particip le	Conditional
Do I study ?	Am I studying?	Will I study ?	Have I studied ?	Would I study ?

Will I be studying ?   Was I studying?

Do I have to study?   Have I been studying?

Would have I studied ?   Did I study ?

Questions (Translate)

Example: Escribir (Infinitive Verb) <u>To write</u>　　　　　　　The Four Templates

Present	**Gerund**	**Future**	**Past Participle**	**Conditional**
Do I write?	Am I writing?	Will I write?	Have I written?	Would I write?

Will I be writing ?　　　　　Was I writing?　　　　　　　Do I have to write? Have I been writing ?

Would have I written ?　　　Did I write?

Example: Leer (Infinitive Verb) <u>To read</u>　　　　　　　The Four Templates

Present	**Gerund**	**Future**	**Past Participle**	**Conditional**
Do I read?	Am I reading?	Will I read?	Have I read?	Would I read?

Will I be reqading ?　　　　　Was I reading?　　　　　　　Do I have to read? Have I been reading ?

Would I have read ?　　　　　Did I read?

Questions (Translate)

Example: Hacer (Infinitive Verb) <u>To do</u>   **The Four Templates**

Present	Gerund	Future	Past Particip le	Conditional
Do I do?	Am I doing?	Will I do?	Have I done ?	Would I do?

Will I be doing ?	Was I doing?		Do I have to do?	Have I been doing ?
Would I have done? ?	Did I do?			

Example: Trabajar (Infinitive Verb) <u>To work</u>   **The Four Templates**

Present	Gerund	Future	Past Particip le	Conditional
Do I work ?	Am I working?	Will I work ?	Have I worked ?	Would I work ?

Will I be working ?	Was I working?		Do I Have to work?	Have I been working ?
Would Have I worked ?	Did I work ?			

Spanish Vocabulary

Spanish Vocabulary

A

A little: Poco, Poquito
A: Un, Uno, Una, Unos, Unas
A lot: Mucho
About: Acerca de
Above: Arriba de
Ache: Dolor
Address: Dirección
Airport: Aeropuerto
After: Después
Afternoon: La tarde
Afterwards: Luego, después
Again: De nuevo,
nuevamente
Ago: Hace
Aid: Ayuda
Air: Aire
Airline: Aerolínea
Airplane: Avión
All: Todo
Almost: Casi
Alone: Solo
Already: Listo
Also: También
Always: Siempre
Amusing: Divertido
And: Y
Annoy: Molestia, desagrado
Another: Otro

Anybody: Cualquiera
Anyone: Quien quiera
Apple: Manzana
April: Abril
Arrest: Arresto
Arrival: Llegada
At (Place): En la, en el
At (Hour): A las
Automobile: Automóvil
Autumn: Otoño
Awful: Desagradable, horrible
August: Agosto

B

Baggage: Equipaje
Bad: Malo
Baked: Horneado
Bakery: Panadería
Bank: Banco
Barely: Casi
Bargains: Rebajas
Bathroom: Baño
Because: Porque
Bed: Cama
Bed Cover: Cubrecamas
Beef: Carne
Beer: Cerveza
Behind: Detrás de
Between: Entre (medio)
Bicycle: Bicicleta

Black: Negro
Blood: Sangre
Blue: Azul
Boat: Bote, barco
Book: Libro
Boss: Jefe
Bottle: Botella
Box: Caja
Boy: Niño
Bread: Pan
Breakdown: Ruptura
Breakfast: Desayuno
British: Británico
Brown: Marrón
Bulb: Bombillo
Bull: Toro
Bus: Autobús
Busy: Ocupado
But: Pero
Butter: Mantequilla
Button: Botón
By the way: A propósito

C

Calf: Ternero, becerro
Canteen: Cantina
Car: Auto, vehículo
Careful: Cuidado
Cart: Carrito
Caution: Atención, cautela

Spanish Vocabulary

Cents: Céntimos, Centavos
Cereal: Cereal
Change: Cambio
Cheap: Barato
Cheese: Queso
Cherry: Cereza
Chest: Pecho
Chicken: Pollo
Child: Niño
Chocolate: Chocolate
Church: Iglesia
Cigarette Lighter: Encendedor
Clean: Limpio
Clock: Reloj
Clothes: Ropa
Class: Clase
Close: Cerrar
Coat: Abrigo
Coal: Carbon
Coffee: Café
Cold: Frío
Complete: Completo
Concert: Concierto
Corner: Esquina
Cream: Crema
Cup: Taza
Curve: Curva
Customs: Aduana

D

Daily: Diario, Cotidiano
Ladies: Damas
Dance: Baile
Danger: Peligro
Dark: Oscuro
Day: Día
Dead: Muerto
Dear: Querido
December: Diciembre
Dentist: Dentista
Department Store: Tienda, Almacén
Departure: Salida, Partida
Dinner: Cena
Discount: Descuento
Desert: Desierto
Despite: A pesar de
Dessert: Postre
Detour: Desvío
Diapers: Pañales
Dictionary: Diccionario
Dining room: Comedor
Dirty: Sucio
Dizzy: Aturdido
Down: Abajo
Dozen: Docena
Dress: Vestido
Drip (Leak): Goteo
Drugstore: Farmacia

E

Each: Cada
Early: Temprano
Egg: Huevo
Either: Cualquiera
Electricity: Electricidad
Eleven: Once
Embassy: Embajada
Emergency: Emergencia
Empty: Vacío
England: Inglaterra
Entrance: Entrada
Error: Error
Evening: Noche
Even though: Aún cuando
Every: Cada
Everybody: Todos, todas
Exchange: Cambio
Excursion: Excursión
Excuse (me): Perdóname
Exit: Salida
Expensive: Caro, costoso
Eye: Ojo
Eye Glasses: Lentes

F

Fair: Feria, justo
Family: Familia
Far: Lejos

Spanish Vocabulary

Fast: Rápido
Father: Padre
Faucet: Grifo
Fault: Culpa, Falta
February: Febrero
Fever: Fiebre
Film: Película
Fine: Bueno
Fire: Fuego
First: Primero
Fish: Pescado
Flag: Bandera
Flight: Vuelo, escape
Fly: Mosca
Food: Comida
Foot: Pie
For: Para
Forbidden: Prohibido
Fork: Tenedor
Forty: Cuarenta
Four: Cuatro
Fourteen: Catorce
Fourth: Cuarto
Free: Gratis, libre
Fresh water: Agua fresca
Friday: Viernes
Fried: Frito
Friend: Amigo
Friendly: Amable, amistoso

From: De
Fruit: Fruta
Funny: Cómico

G

Game: Juego
Garlic: Ajo
Gas: Gas
Gasoline: Gasolina
Generally: Generalmente
Gentleman: Caballero, Señor
Gift: Regalo
Girl: Muchacha, niña
Glove: Guante
Good: Bueno
Gray: Gris
Green: Verde
Greetings: Saludos
Guide: Guía

H

Half: Medio, Mitad
Ham: Jamón
Handbag: Bolsa, Cartera
Happy: Feliz
Headache: Dolor de cabeza
Heart: Corazón
Heat: Calor
Heavy: Pesado
Hello: Hola

Help: Ayuda
Here: Aquí
Hospital: Hospital
Hot: Caliente
Hour: Hora
How: Cómo
How far: A qué distancia
How long: Cuánto tiempo
How much: Cuánto
Hot: Caliente
Hundred: Ciento
Husband: Esposo, marido

I

Ice cream: Helado
If: Si
Immediately: Inmediatamente
In: En
Included: Incluido
Infant: Bebé
Information: Información
Inside: Dentro, Adentro
Introduce: Presentar

J

Jam: Mermelada
January: Enero
Jewelry: Joyas
Juice: Jugo
July: Julio

Spanish Vocabulary

K

Keep: Mantener
Key: Llave
Kind: Amable, Agradable
Kitchen: Cocina
Knife: Cuchillo

L

Lady: Dama
Large: Grande
Last: Lo último, la última
Late: Tarde
Lavatory: Lavabo, excusado
Laxative: Laxante
Least: Menos
Leather: Cuero
Left: Izquierda
Legal: Legal
Lemon: Limón
Lemonade: Limonada
Less: Menos
Letter: Carta
Lettuce: Lechuga
List: Lista
Little: Pequeño
Low: Bajo
Lunch: Almuerzo

N

Nothing: Nada
Notice: Aviso
November: Noviembre
Now: Ahora
Number: Número

M

Machine: Maquina
Madam: Señora
Made in: Hecho en
Magazine: Revista
Mail: Correo
Manager: Gerente
Many: Muchos
Map: Mapa
March: Marzo
Matches: Cerillas, fósforos
May: Mayo
May be: Quizás
Meal: Comida
Men: Hombre
Merely: Casi, apenas
Meat: Carne
Menu: Menú
Message: Mensaje
Middle: Medio, mitad
Midnight: Medianoche
Milk: Leche

Minute: Minuto
Miss: Señorita
Mister: Señor
Monday: Lunes
Money: Dinero
Money Order: Giro postal
Month: Mes
Morning: Mañana
Mother: Madre
Motocycle: Moto
Movie: Película
Mr.: Señor
Mrs.: Señora
Much: Mucho
Museum: Museo

N

Napkin: Servilleta
Nationality: Nacionalidad
Naturally: Naturalmente
Near: Cerca de
Neither: Ninguno
Never: Nunca
Next: Próximo
Next to: Al lado de
Night: Noche
Nightclub: Cabaret
Nine: Nueve
Nineteen: Diez y nueve
Ninety: Noventa

Spanish Vocabulary

Ninth: Noveno
No: No
Noise: Ruido
None: Ninguno
Noon: Mediodía
Not: No

O

October: Octubre
Of course: Por supuesto
Office: Oficina
Often: A menudo
Okay: Está bien
Omelet: Tortilla
On: En, sobre
Once: Una vez
One: Un
One Hundred: Cien
Only: Solamente
On sale: En venta
Open: Abierto
Orange: Naranja
Otherwise: De otra manera
Outside: Fuera
Over: Sobre
Overcoat: Abrigo

P

Portero: Porter
Puede Ser: It can be

Panadería: Bakery Pañales:
Diapers
Papá: Father
Para: For
Pare: Stop
Pareciera: Seemingly
Parece: Seems like Parque:
Park
Pasaje: Ticket
Papas: Potatoes
Papel higiénico: Toilet paper
Paraguas: Umbrella
Pasaporte: Passport
Payment: Pago
Película: Movie
Pequeño: Small, Little
Por día: Per day
Por supuesto: Of course
Postre: Dessert Perdóneme:
Excuse me Pero: But
Pesado: Heavy
Pasajero: Passenger

Q

Querido: Dear
Queso: Cheese
Quizás: Maybe
Que: What, that

R

Radiador: Radiator

Railroad: Ferrocarril, Tren
Rain: Lluvia
Raincoat: Impermeable
Razor Blade: Hojilla de
afeitar
Ready: Listo
Receipt: Recibo
Record: Registro
Red: Rojo
Repeat: Repita
Reserved: Reservado
Rest Room: Lavabo, Baño
Rice: Arroz
Right: Derecho, Derecha
Right away: Enseguida
Right now: Ahora mismo
Roast Beef: Rosbif
Roasted: Asado
Round Trip: Ida y vuelta

S

Salad: Ensalada
Sale: Venta
Salty: Salado
Saturday: Sábado
School: Escuela
Seat: Asiento
Second: Segundo
See you later: Hasta luego
September: Septiembre

Spanish Vocabulary

Service: Servicio
Seven: Siete
Seventh: Séptimo
Seventeen: Diez y siete
Seventy: Setenta
Several: Varios
Shebert: Sorbete
Ship: Barco
Shopping: Ir de compras
Show Me: Muéstrame
Shower: Ducha
Shrimp: Camarón
Sick: Enfermo
Sir: Señor
Six: Seis
Sixteen: Diez y seis
Sixth: Sexto
Sixty: Sesenta
Slow: Despacio
Small: Pequeño
Smoker: Fumador
Snack: Bocadillo
Soap: Jabón
Soon: Pronto
Soup: Sopa
Somebody: Alguien
Someone: Alguien
Spoon: Cuchara

Sports: Deportes
Spring: Resorte
Spring (season): Primavera
Station: Estación
Stewardess: Azafata
Sticker: Etiqueta
Still: Todavía
Stop: Alto, pare, deténgase
Store: Tienda
Strawberry: Fresa
Street: Calle
Subway: Metro
Sugar: Azúcar
Suitcase: Maleta
Summer: Verano
Sunday: Domingo
Sure: Seguro

T

Table: Mesa
Tablet: Comprimido, Tableta
Tailor: Sastre
Tap: Grifo
Tea: Té
Teaspoon: Cucharita
Telegram: Telegrama
Telephone: Teléfono
Television: Televisión
Ten: Diez

Thank you: Gracias
Theft: Robo
There: Allá
There is/are: Hay
Thermometer: Termómetro
Thief: Ladrón
Thing: Cosa
Third: Tercero
Thirteen: Trece
Thirty: Treinta
This evening: Esta noche
Thousand: Mil
Three: Tres
Through: A través
Thursday: Jueves
Tuesday: Martes
Ticket: Boleto
Time (Hour): Hora
Timetable: Horario
Tip (gratuity): Propina
To: A
Toast (bread): Pan
Tabacco: Tabaco
Today: Hoy
Toilet paper: Papel higiénico
Toilet: Excusado, lavabo
Tomorrow: Mañana
Tonight: Esta noche
Too (Also): También

Spanish Vocabulary

Tourism: Turismo
Tourist: Turista
Towel: Toalla
Track: Pista
Traffic: Tráfico
Train: Tren
Tuesday: Martes
TV Set: Televisor
Twelve: Doce
Twenty: Veinte
Twice: Dos veces
Two: Dos
Two hundred:
Doscientos
Typewriter: Máquina de Escribir

U

Umbrella: Paraguas
Under: Debajo
Underneath: Debajo de
Understood: Entendido
United States: Estados Unidos
Until: Hasta
Up: Arriba
Urgent: Urgente
Unless: A menos que
Unwilling: Sin voluntad

V

Vacant: Disponible
Valuable: De valor

Vanilla: Vainilla
Veal: Ternera
Vegetables:
Legumbres, vegetales
Very: Muy
Vinegar: Vinagre

W

Waiter: Mesonero, mesero
Waitress: Mesonera, mesera
Waiting Room: Sala de espera
Wallet: Billetera, cartera
Warm: Caliente
Watch out: Cuidado
Water: Agua
Watermelon: Sandía
Wednesday: Miércoles
Week: Semana
Weekly: Semanal
Welcome: Bienvenidos
Well: Bien
Wet paint: Recién pintado,
pintura fresca
What: Qué, cuál
When: Cuándo
Whenever: Cuando sea
Where: Dónde
Where to: Adonde
Wherever: Donde sea
Which: Cuál

Whichever: Cualquiera que sea
White: Blanco
Who: Quien
Whoever: Quien quiera que sea
Whom: A quien
Whose: De quien
Why: Por qué
Wide: Ancho
Wife: Esposa
Willing: Ganas,
voluntad, deseo
Window: Ventana
Wine: Vino
Winter: Invierno
With: Con
Woman: Mujer
Women: Mujeres
Word: Palabra
Wristwatch: Reloj

Y

Year: Año
Yellow: Amarillo
Yes: Sí
Yesterday: Ayer
Yet: Todavía
Yield: Ceder el paso

Z

Zipper: Cierre

Notes

1- <u>Gerund / (Gerundio):</u> Verb in Gerund required the verb " To Be" to preceed them, in Spanish that would the verb " Estar". To practice building phrases in Gerund (Action), simply place the Verb To Be ("Estar") just before the Gerund Verb using the following conjugations.

(I – Am) – Yo – Estoy
(You – Are) – Usted – Esta
(He – is) – El – Esta
(She – is) – Ella – Esta
(We – Are) – Nosotro – Estamos
(You – Are) – Ustedes – Estan
(They – Are) – Ellos – Estan
(IT – is) – Eso/Ello – Esta

<u>Ejemplos:</u>

Yo estoy escribiendo – I Am Writing
Usted está esperando – You Are Waiting
El está llamando – He is Calling
Ella está cocinando – She Is Cooking
Nosotros estamos cocinando – We Are Eating
Ustedes están comiendo – You Are Eating
Ellos están viniendo – They Are Coming

Notes

2-Participle (Participio): Verbs in Participle require the verb "To Have" to preceed them, in Spanish that would be the verb "Haber". To practice building phrases in Gerund (Past), simply place the Verb To Have ("Haber") just before the Participle Verb using the following conjugations:

I – Am) – Yo – He
(You – Are) – Usted – Ha
(He – is) – El – Ha
(She – is) – Ella – Ha
(We – Are) – Nosotro – Hemos
(You – Are) – Ustedes – Han
(They – Are) – Ellos – Han
(IT – is) – Eso/Ello – Ha

Examples:
Yo He Esperado – I have Waited
Usted Ha recibido Correo – You Have Gotten Mail
Ella Ha Dormido Bien – She Has Slept Well
El Ha Comido Tarde – He Has Eaten Late
Nosotros Hemos corrido en la mañana: We have run in the morning
Ustedes Han ido a Clases temprano – You have gone to class early
Ellos Han Hecho La Tarea Juntos – They Have dode the Homework together

Notes

In Spanish you use the letter "A" between infinitive verbs.

Examples:

Yo puedo ir a comer mas tarde
I can go to eat later

Yo quiero venir a visitarlos la semana proxima
I want to come to visit you next week

I have to go to eat
Yo Tengo Que ir "a" comer

www.ingramcontent.com/pod-product-compliance
Lightning Source LLC
Chambersburg PA
CBHW082108120626
46553CB00011B/3598